Enjoy the book, Tie some, and catch some big ones!

Stu

TYED & TRUE

101 fly patterns proven to catch fish

STU THOMPSON

Suite 300 - 990 Fort St
Victoria, BC, V8V 3K2
Canada

www.friesenpress.com

Copyright © 2021 by Stu Thompson
First Edition — 2021

All rights reserved.

No part of this publication may be reproduced in any form, or by any means, electronic or mechanical, including photocopying, recording, or any information browsing, storage, or retrieval system, without permission in writing from FriesenPress.

ISBN
978-1-03-910247-7 (Hardcover)
978-1-03-910246-0 (Paperback)
978-1-03-910248-4 (eBook)

1. *Sports & Recreation, Fishing*

Distributed to the trade by The Ingram Book Company

For my wife, Rebecca, who has shown me
patience, love, and understanding throughout my fishing life.

TYED & TRUE

"In Tyed and True Stu has applied to perfection the same "demystify and simplify" approach to tying 101 patterns. Presented with a book of fly patterns that lists easy to find materials, offers clear and simple tying instructions, provides guidance on how to fish a pattern, and which species can be targeted with it, includes a large portion of multiple species flies that can be tied in minutes, and to top it off contains patterns that have all proven successful time and again, I will not just call such a book a great deal, it is a steal. If you owned Tyed and True chances are that it will become the book sitting closest to your tying bench, it will be so for me, not because it is the latest book but because I know from having tied and fished several of Stu's patterns that it represents a pretty sure path to success."

—Marcel Duval, Lieutenant-General (Retired) Royal Canadian Air Force, fly fisher, fly tier, and passionate bamboo rod maker

"Stu's book is full of many quality images showing anglers with a range of fish species and a close up of the fly that shows every thread of detail. The exceptional photos allow the beginner or veteran fly tier the ability to discern and dissect the materials in conjunction with excellent step by step instructions."

—Kirk Dietrich author of "Tying Bugs"

"Stu Thompson fly fishes for trout. We all do. But he also fishes for "unconventional" fly rod fish like walleye, carp, sauger, drum – wait for it – channel cats. Stu shows you 101 of the fly patterns you'll need with clear instructions on how to tie them, along the way revealing the insights and innovations of a life-long fly tier."

—Jim McLennan author of "Trout Streams of Alberta, Blue Ribbon Bow, Fly Fishing Western Trout Streams, and Water Marks"

"Must say, I was very impressed with the book – it's going to be a winner. The fact it talks about tying for fish other than just trout puts it leap years ahead of virtually every other book."

—Ken Bailey Hunting editor of "Outdoor Canada" Magazine and author of "No Place Like Home"

"Stu Thompson is a skilled fly fisher and superb tier. His works of art are a pleasure to tie and fish. Tyed and True is a breath of fresh air. You will treasure it for the rest of your life."

—Gord Pyzer, Canadian Angler Hall of Fame, National Freshwater Fishing Hall of Fame, and Canadian Outdoor Hall of Fame

"Tyed and True is an innovative and diverse compendium of 101 fly patterns that represent a menu of flies the author has either developed himself, or inspired and created by fellow anglers. In my opinion, these patterns are hallmarks of a master angler and fly tier."

—John Nishi, member of Fly Fishing Team Canada

"If you enjoy fly tying and fly fishing for a wide variety of fish species, you're sure to find Stu Thompson's new fly tying book an extremely helpful and insightful resource. Stu's use of both traditional and modern fly tying materials and techniques, has led to the creation of some very innovative fly patterns. This book is sure to please and inspire fly tiers and fly fishers across North America and abroad."

—Todd Oishi, member of Fly Fishing Team Canada and President of Fly Fishing Canada

"Stu has done a fantastic job of assembling his own recognized patterns plus those of other anglers. This is not just another fly tying book; this is a catalogue of truly effective fly patterns that really work. I strongly recommend the book to anyone who wants to "up their game" in terms of new fly patterns that are "combat proven" and will definitely help catch more fish!"

—Colin McKeown, host/producer of The New Fly Fisher

"Stu Thompson's meticulously tested fly patterns are simple, highly original and catch fish like crazy. In this must-have book, he generously shares them with the rest of us. The photos are superb, the tying instructions are straightforward and, even better, include something most fly-pattern books neglect: actual real-world fishing advice for every fly. Rather than gathering dust on a shelf, Tyed and True will spend its life wide open, well-thumbed and sitting beside your fly-tying vise.

—Scott Gardner, associate editor and fly fishing columnist, Outdoor Canada magazine

"Stu's keen enthusiasm, interest, and understanding of trout, and alternate species on the fly rod has made him stand apart from most fly anglers. Stu has always been of the belief that fish behavior, with location, and quality presentations of well tied flies is the success of the angler for any species. This book is well needed for both the tier and the angler."

—Gary Hanke, author, member of Fly Fishing Team Canada, Canadian representative for Semperfl, Hends Products, Stonfo, and Renome Scissors, and gold medal winner of the German Open Fly Tying Championship

"Stu and me are like minded, both believing if a fish eats aquatic insects, baitfish, and other invertebrates, it can be taken on a fly rod. He ties his flies designed to catch a variety of fish, not to impress other fly fishers with their looks. When I am heading out on the water I always have an assortment of Stu's flies within my fly box including his Easter Egg Bugger for walleye and the Weedman's Slider for chasing pike. My personal best pike, a 49-inch monster from Saskatchewan's Reindeer Lake came on a black Weedman's. Stu graciously passes along his insight, tying tips and presentation recommendations so you can get the most out of each pattern. I highly recommend adding Tyed and True to your fly tying library so you can experience more on the water enjoyment and success."

—Phil Rowley, author of The Orvis Guide to Stillwater Trout Fishing, Fly Patterns for Stillwaters, and Stillwater Selections, and co-host of The New Fly Fisher

CONTENTS

Acknowledgements	i
Foreword	iii
Introduction	iv

CHIRONOMIDS — 1

R & B Tom	2
Red Tom	3
Clear Tom	4
Summer Duck Chironomid	5
Fur Midge	7
Stu's Orange Chromie	9
Stu's Chromie	10
CB Midge Black	11
CB Midge Wire	12
Red Bead Midge	13

NYMPHS — 15

Rebecca's Damsel	16
Darkwater Damsel	17
'52 Buick	18
Jen Dragon	19
Bodacious Dragon	
Fly Nymph	20
Huff 'n Fluff Dragon	22
Darkwater Swimmer	23
Nixon's Nymph	24
Stu's Backswimmer	25
Floating Backswimmer	26
Abbott's Costello	28

Owen's Golden Retriever	29
Elastic Band Caddis	30
FFA Caddis Emerger	32
Manitoba Mayfly	33
Cheater's Caddis	34
FFA Stonefly	36
Derek's Demon Stone	38
Corrigan's Craw	40
The Muncher	43
Calli Nymph	45
Stu's Sow Bug	47
The Tick	48
Beck's Hex	50

WET FLIES — 53

Mark's Pink Bead Fly	54
Sally Soft Hackle	55
GH Wet Fly	56
Grouse and Orange	57
Grouse and Green	58
Mrs. Simpson	60
Drunken Nymph	61

DRY FLIES — 63

Mike's Mayfly	64
Mike's Parachute Mayfly	66
Mike's Hexagenia	68

POPPERS — 71

Mikey Mouse	72
Steve's Slider	74
The Leaf	75
SE Foam Popper	76
Tiger's Tail Popper	78
Jig-A-Pop	80
Kermit	82
The Terminator	84
Bass Diver	85

STEAMERS — 87

The Blob	88
Becky's Black Strip Leech	90
Pink Zonker	91
Easter Egg Bugger	93
The Sawich Killer	94
Claret Tiger Leech	96
Myminnow	97
Derose Dace	98
Mallard SB	100
Bendback Minnow Black And Orange	103
Whatizit	104
Erickson's Clouser	105
Kevin's Leech	106
Tokaryk Killer	107
DDH Leech	109
Red River Shiner	110
SRT Stickleback	111
Bou Bug	112
Erickson's Dream	114
Stu's Sculpin	116
Zeke's Nightmare	118
Brigette's Badass Baitfish	121
Manitoba Matuka	122
Rolled Muddler	123
Lockport Standard	124

DDH Eyes Natural Grey	125
DDH Eyes White Minnow	128
DDH Head Purple And Pink	130

PIKE AND MUSKY STREAMERS — 133

CG's Minnow	134
Hillbilly Baba	135
TGT Streamer	136
Bunny Leech	137
Green Zacattack	138
Red River Sculpin	140
P & W Pike Muddler	143
Weedman's Slider	144
Winter's Storm	146
KT's Baitfish	148
Zonker Minnow Perch	150
Super Cisco	152
Perch Zacattack	156
SR Yellow Red Head	158
Black & Chartreuse Casper	160
Mike's Goldfish	162
Rain Drop	164
RC's Punch Fly	166
Sinfield's Musky Killer	168
Sinfield's Zonker	170
TJ's folly	173
TJ's Folly Two	174
Craft Fur Popsicle	176
Keith's Flatwing Streamer	178
Steve's Sheep Deceiver	179
Species Taken on the DDH Leech	183
Appendix	183
Essential Tools for Beginners	184
How to Make a Dubbing Loop	188
How to Card Yarn	190
Glossary	192
Final Thoughts	195
Index—Chronological Order	196
Index—Alphabetical Order	198

ACKNOWLEDGEMENTS

I am truly blessed." That's what I tell myself every time I do something and it works out. I believe people are put into your life for a reason, whether in friendship, in collaboration on a project, or simply to help through the rough spots. It is a mystery, as these people appear to show up at the precise moment when needed most. Such is the case with this book and the people that have helped in the process and production. This book would not be here without their help and for that I truly thank them as it has been a dream of mine for many years.

The first two people I would like to thank are Stephen Jay and Steve Erickson. They have been with me through thick and thin, and the contribution of their favorite patterns, ongoing feedback, and encouragement on this venture has been invaluable.

Mike "Zeke" Corrigan is another friend who is not only an exceptional tier, as witnessed by his fly patterns, but has freely given his time in critiquing both manuscript and tying steps. Thank you.

In addition, I would like to thank Ken Sawich and Keith Sinfield who also supplied their favorite patterns which work and are worth fishing.

Appreciation and thanks to Angela Dobler for doing the first edit to my manuscript. She gave me great insights and understanding to the publishing business.

Thank you to Phil Monahan, of the Orvis Fly Fishing Blog, who not only fishes my flies, he also tries my experimental patterns. In addition, he supplied a few excellent photographs for use in this book.

Scott Gardner, Associate Editor of Outdoor Canada Magazine, who, although doesn't realize it, spurred me on to complete this pattern book and supplied me with some tremendous photos. Thank you.

Many thanks to Andrew Crozier whose abilities in the graphic arts field and artistic flair helped design the cover for this book. It's just unbelievable how much talent he has.

To one of the best fly fishermen I know and good friend, Jeff Currier, thank you for writing the forward to my book. Looking forward to your next 39-inch Channel Cat.

A big thanks to all the people of Friesen Press who took the time to answer my questions and to see this book to publication.

I would also like to thank all the people who allowed me to use their photographs. Without them this book would have a very different look.

Most of all I would like to thank my family for believing in me and this book. Without your support and love it would have been extremely hard to finish this. Thank you.

I have been truly blessed.

Stu Thompson

Jeff Currier with a huge rainbow.
Photo courtesy of Jeff Currier

FOREWORD

I've been in the fly fishing industry for a long time. I've watched new products evolve, been part of exploring new destinations and seen a ton of people come and go. I've also been lucky to meet and become friends with some of the finest fly designers on the planet. Some of them will always stand out more than others.

So who was this fun, gregarious, smiling guy tying flies at the fishing shows? The flies were cutting edge and they caught my eye. These weren't simply pretty flies; these were flies to catch fish. The patterns were creative and weren't only for trout – this dude had flies for bass, carp, and even channel catfish! I had to meet him.

The knowledgeable fly fisher was Stu Thompson. I'd soon wiggle my way through the spectators to his tying table. Stu spotted the glimmer in my eye and we were quick to talk. After five minutes of chatting I could tell Stu was the kind of person who was a new friend for life.

I got to know Stu well over the next few show seasons and indeed we became good friends. We had a great time talking fishing. We'd start about trout but soon we would veer to pike, carp, and every so often, channel cats.

"You catch big channel cats on flies?", I asked.

"I do and you need to come do it with me Jeff!", Stu spoke loud in a serious tone.

That was it. You invite me to fly fish for a fish as unique and big as a channel catfish, I'm coming. What made the visit easy was that at the time I was the host of the Warmwater segments of Fly Fish T.V. When I suggested a show on the Red River in Manitoba with Stu Thompson, the Fly Fish TV team was on board.

I'll never forget the trip up to Manitoba. The weather was terrible when we landed in Winnipeg. It looked like the city was flooded. Stu met us at the baggage claim with a big grin, "We have our work cut out, but fish love water."

High water has crushed many a trip and I thought this would be another. But Stu didn't think so, and we headed for the Red River. The Red was chocolate-red and raging far above its banks. For a guy that comes from clear flowing blue ribbon trout streams, I thought we were doomed. Stu laughed and simply said, "They don't call it the Red for nothing".

Stu's positive attitude and knowledge of fly fishing the Red River was amazing. He got me started with one of his custom flies, the DDH Minnow, and explained how the bead eyes of the fly would make some noise and that's how the cats were going to key onto the fly in the muddy water. Boy was he right. Despite these tough conditions we caught several huge channel cats, common carp, freshwater drum, sauger, and Stu caught the first big mouth buffalo I'd ever seen.

Stu Thompson has compiled a book of fly patterns that catch fish in Manitoba, the rest of Canada, and honestly I not only use these flies at home in Idaho, but I take them all over the world. This book is full of tricks and tips and stories to go with. Now kick back, enjoy the read and spin some of Stu's favorite Manitoba fly patterns.

Jeff Currier
Jeff Currier Global Fly Fishing

A typical freshwater drum caught on a Red River Shiner. The great thing about these fish is that they will readily strike a fly.

INTRODUCTION

We fly tyers are an amazing lot, aren't we? Sitting at our vice for hours trying to come up with that one exceptional fly, which will work for just about anything that has fins. Better still, designing new flies with new materials that are flashier, brighter, and downright irresistible to fish and to other fly fishers.

What about spending hours tying up a traditional salmon pattern or making realistic flies? My hat is off to these folks; they have quite a bit of patience and a lot of artistic ability. As for this old bean, I prefer to keep things on the simpler side. My flies are not that difficult to tie, but they are designed so I can tie 12 of one pattern in an hour.

I know what some of you may wonder, "How can this guy tie a dozen flies in an hour?" I hate to admit it but I am a production tyer. I prefer working with one material at a time and doing one step at a time. That is if I'm doing a dozen bucktail streamers then I will do 12 tinsel bodies first then work on the wing. This is just my style of tying. As for some of my designs—simple flies catch fish, period. Nothing has to be fancy; all you need is a fair representation of the food item you want to imitate and then go and catch fish.

Now with all of that said, there are a couple of patterns that I cannot make a dozen in an hour but only six because of the number of steps required to tie these flies. So I would say that these patterns are a little harder to tie. But once you discover the procedure to tie these flies, it does become easier.

With that thought in mind, I believe that size and silhouette are the main reasons fish will hit a fly. The next important item is colour—not a solid colour mind you—but a mixture of colours. There is nothing on God's earth that is one solid colour. When you pick up a nymph and hold it in your hand it appears to be one colour. Put that same nymph in a small white container with water and you will notice small subtle changes in the way it looks. A brown mayfly nymph in your hand will look totally brown, but in a white container there are hues of tan, grey, and brown. What a difference!

Since 1974, I have been mixing and blending different colours of dubbing to use in my flies. I use colours to make colours; that is, my brown dubbing has no brown in it at all. It is a blend of four different colours to make brown and with these four colours I can go from a sunrise type of orange to an amazing rich, deep chocolate brown.

Since I started this crazy journey (in 1965, to be exact) I have tied thousands upon thousands of flies. Some have worked extremely well and others not so well, but all the flies in this book have caught fish—and some really nice ones as well.

Some of you will say, "How come there aren't more dry flies?" The answer to that question is simple: 95 percent of the fish's diet is underneath the surface of the water and only five percent is on the surface. The flies in this book represent that thought. I don't know about you but I love catching fish so why would I use a dry fly when there are no insects hatching?

Not only that, but just about every hatch in my home province occurs in the late evening and goes into the night. In other words, from about 10 p.m. until 2 or 3 a.m. If you aren't used to fishing these hours, there is not a lot of fly fishing available. And fly fishing in the dark does have its drawbacks, especially with a black-and-white animal that loves to investigate anyone walking along shorelines. The aroma is out of this world!

You will also notice a few flies with different names attached to them. These are tied by some very well-respected individuals who, in turn, have become very admired friends, and their flies catch some REALLY BIG fish. I do not pretend to be an originator of all these patterns, for I have had some help from some great tyers through the years. There are some patterns out in the world that are similar to the ones in the book, but let me assure you I have not copied any flies from anyone, nor would I. For some fly patterns, I have given credit where it is due. Tyers like Sylvester Nemes, Dan Blanton, and others have helped and shown me how to tie some of these flies. I have changed some of the colours and materials for the species of fish I want to catch.

Some of the flies in this book are so easy to tie it's unbelievable, but some others are more complex. Let me say this: once you know the procedures, all flies are simple to tie. What you will find in this book are flies that have been proven to catch multiple species of fish anywhere in the world.

Enjoy,
Stu Thompson

CHIRONOMIDS

2   **R & B TOM**

3   **RED TOM**

4   **CLEAR TOM**

5   **SUMMER DUCK CHIRONOMID**

7   **FUR MIDGE**

9   **STU'S ORANGE CHROMIE**

10   **STU'S CHROMIE**

11   **CB MIDGE BLACK**

12   **CB MIDGE WIRE**

13   **RED BEAD MIDGE**

Easy

Moderate

Difficult

CHIRONOMIDS

One of the smallest aquatic insects, it makes up to 70 percent of a fish's diet, hence it is one of the most important to imitate.

The author with a 25-in (63-cm) rainbow from his favourite trout lake.

R & B TOM

MATERIALS

Designed by Stu Thompson

Thread: Semperfli Nano Silk, 6/0, black; and 3/0, red

Hook: Daiichi 1550, size 10-18

Body: Semperfli Nano Silk, 6/0, black and 3/0, red

Head: Peacock herl

1. Place the hook in the vice and start the black thread at the eye of the hook.
2. Tie in the red thread and wrap the black thread to the point of the barb.
3. Advance the thread to the eye of the hook and then back towards the point of the barb, stopping 5 turns past the barb. Take the black thread back to the eye of the hook. Please note: all the wraps have to be touching.
4. Wrap the red thread as a rib doing 3 to 4 turns along the hook shank.
5. Tie off the red thread and tie in 2 to 3 pieces of peacock herl. Wrap the herl forward, tying off at the eye.
6. Form the head and whip finish. The fly is complete.

STU'S TIPS Basically designed for trout, I have found another species of fish that just love midges. Lake Cisco (aka tullibee) have a great fondness for this pattern. Cisco do not grow that large and when you catch a 16-incher (40 cm), that is an enormous fish and you can put a feather in your cap. When fishing this pattern in a river, I will always drift through a back eddy as often as I can. Tullibee love holding on the edges and will hit midges as they drift by giving us fly anglers a terrific opportunity.

RED TOM

MATERIALS

Designed by Stu Thompson

Thread: Semperfli Nano Silk, 6/0, black; and 3/0, red

Hook: Daiichi 1550, size 10-18

Body: Semperfli Nano Silk, 3/0 red

Head: Peacock herl

1. Place the hook in the vice and start the red thread at the eye of the hook.
2. Wrap the thread back to the point of the barb in close-touching wraps.
3. After reaching a quarter of the way down the bend of the hook, advance the thread back to the eye of the hook in close-touching wraps.
4. Keep wrapping the thread until a nicely tapered body is formed.
5. Whip finish the red thread and trim off.
6. Place the fly in a piece of foam and apply a coat of head cement. (Do 5 to 6 coats on each body allowing the head cement to dry in between.)
7. Place the hook back in the vice and attach the black thread at the eye of the hook.
8. Select a strand of peacock herl and tie in.
9. Wrap the herl 5 to 6 times and tie off.
10. Form the head and the fly is complete.

STU'S TIPS Looking at my midges, everyone asks: "Do they really work?" All I can say is "Absolutely!" which is true and for a lot more species other than trout. At times, people fall into a narrow path of belief. This fly will only catch such and such when that is not the case. Think about it: since both the fish and the aquatic insects live in the water, doesn't it make sense that no matter what species of fish, they all eat the same food? So why don't more fly fishermen try for different species on the fly? After all isn't that why we go fishing, to catch fish on a fly? Try this pattern for different species—you may well be surprised.

CLEAR TOM

MATERIALS

Designed by Stu Thompson

Thread: Clear mono (invisible thread); and Semperfli Nano Silk, 6/0, black

Hook: Daiichi 1550, size 10-18

Body: Clear mono

Head: Peacock herl

1. Place the hook in the vice and start the thread at the eye of the hook, wrapping back to a quarter of the way around the bend.
2. Wrap the thread back to the eye of the hook and then wrap back to the bend. Keep on doing this until a nice tapered body takes effect.
3. Whip finish the clear thread at the eye of the hook.
4. Take the hook out of the vice, place it in a piece of foam, and apply a coat of head cement. (I will usually do 3 to 4 dozen midges at a time and do the head cement all at once. Also I will put 4 to 5 coats of cement on the bodies.)
5. After drying, place the hook in the vice and start the black thread at the eye of the hook.
6. Take one strand of peacock herl and tie it in.
7. Do 5 to 6 wraps of the herl and tie it off.
8. Form the head and whip finish.

STU'S TIPS If I remember correctly, I have been tying this pattern for 40 years. It still works—mostly used for trout in early spring. I have also used it for perch, lake whitefish, sauger, goldeye, mooneye, and have had friends catch grayling on them. A dry line and long leader will work wonders for fly fishers. I will also add that using indicators will give the angler an advantage in fishing midges.

SUMMER DUCK CHIRONOMID

MATERIALS

Designed by Brian Chan; tied by Ken Sawich

Thread: UNI-Thread, tan 6/0

Hook: Mustad 37160, size 8-14

Body: Summer Duck midge flex, 1/8 in (0.32 cm) wide

Rib: Silver wire, fine

Bead: White (to match hook size)

1. De-barb the hook and slide the bead on up to the hook eye.
2. Place the hook in the vice and start the thread behind the bead. Wrap a thread base until the mid-point of the bend.
3. Continue wrapping until a tapered body is formed. The thread should be positioned behind the bead.
4. Tie in the silver wire. Wrap the thread to the end of the tapered body, then advance the thread back to the bead.
5. Tie in the Summer Duck midge flex and wrap the thread back to the tapered end of the fly. Once again, advance the thread back behind the bead.
6. Wrap the midge flex forward, close-touching wraps to the bead. Tie off. Note: The tighter you pull on the midge flex, the lighter it becomes.
7. Do 2 to 3 wraps of the wire at the very rear of the body to create a tag, then wrap the wire forward 7 times to make a segmented body.
8. Tie the wire off behind the bead.
9. Build a small head, and whip finish. The fly is complete.

In the pursuit of trout, anything can happen.

KEN'S FISHING LOG "I've had a fair amount of success using this pattern. I fish this midge from spring to fall due to the fact that midges are a staple food item for trout. Using a dry line and a long leader will help getting the fly down to the proper depths where the fish are holding.

"My friend and I were fishing a lake on the west side of Manitoba and after a slow morning we decided to anchor and have lunch. We anchored the boat and dug out our lunches, and I had a brilliant thought while doing this. I rigged both rods with tandem chironomids and cast them out. Of course, there weren't any rod holders in the boat so we just laid them on the bow. After a couple of bites of my sandwich, I noticed a movement. In a millisecond that movement was moving at Mach 2. My rod went flying by my head and I just managed to duck in time. My friend got the trolling motor started and we raced after the rod, but after a quick chase the rod disappeared to the depths below not to be seen again. It's amazing what happens in the fly-fishing community. The story got around about me losing my rod and wouldn't you know it, a couple of weeks later it was returned to me. After telling my part of the story with the second half it turned out to be quite hilarious. Fly fishermen: what a great bunch."

FUR MIDGE

MATERIALS — *Designed by Stu Thompson*

Thread: Semperfli Nano Silk, 8/0, black

Hook: Daiichi 1550, size 10-18

Body: Darkwater Dubbing bloody black

Head: Peacock herl

1. Place the hook in the vice and start the thread at the eye of the hook.
2. Wrap the thread to the point of the barb and let out approximately 2 in (5 cm) of thread.
3. Apply the Darkwater Dubbing to the thread with a twisting motion.
4. Wrap the newly formed dubbing noodle back towards the eye of the hook, stopping approximately 1/16 in (1.5 mm) from the eye.
5. Tie in the peacock herl, do 5 to 6 wraps, then tie off.
6. Form the head and whip finish.

STU'S TIPS Another easily tied fly that produces. This fly can be tied in numerous colours to match any colour of midge that is found in still waters. Basically designed for trout, this pattern has taken lake whitefish, cisco, quillback, perch, and carp. Best colours to use are bloody black, tan, olive, golden olive, and orange.

Kevin Thompson releasing a 24-in (61-cm) rainbow.

STU'S ORANGE CHROMIE

MATERIALS

Designed by Stu Thompson

Thread: Semperfli Nano Silk, 12/0; and monocord, 3/0, fluorescent orange

Hook: Daiichi 1120 or 1550, size 10-18

Body: Monocord, 3/0, fluorescent orange over-wrapped with pearl tinsel

Head: Peacock herl

1. Place the hook in the vice and start the fluorescent orange thread at the eye. With tight turns wrap it to the bend of the hook.
2. Tie in a piece of pearl tinsel and continue to wrap the thread 6 times towards the bend of the hook.
3. After reaching this point, wrap the thread forward to the eye in close-touching wraps. Stop about 1/16 in (1.5 mm) away from the eye.
4. Wrap the pearl tinsel, laying one wrap against another; do not overlap.
5. Tie off the tinsel and whip finish the fluorescent orange thread.
6. Attach the black thread and tie in two pieces of peacock herl. Do 5 to 6 wraps of herl and tie off.
7. Whip finish and the fly is complete.
8. Being a production tyer I will do 3 to 4 dozen bodies and then head cement them 4 to 5 times to build a resilient finish on the body of the fly.

STU'S TIPS What can I say about this fly? One of my favorite colour combinations and it produces, especially when fished tandem with a red & black Tom. There is just something about the body that turns fish on. I have used it in rivers and lakes for a variety of fish with the most challenging being tullibee or what people know as Lake Cisco. It is definitely a difficult situation when fishing in cold weather, but if you are catching 16–17 inch (40–43 cm) tullibee, which is huge, it is very rewarding.

BONUS FLY

STU'S CHROMIE

MATERIALS

Designed by Stu Thompson

Thread: Semperfli Nano Silk, 6/0, black or white (use an olive permanent marker to colour the white thread)

Hook: Daiichi 1120, size 8-18

Body: Flat Mylar silver tinsel

Head: Peacock herl

1. Place the hook in the vice and start the thread at the eye. Leave a long tag end of thread to ensure you have close wraps.
2. Pull up on the tag end so that the thread rests against the previous wrap, ensuring the whole shank of the hook is covered in thread and keeping the same diameter throughout.
3. Once the bend of the hook is reached, cut the tag end of thread and tie in the flat silver tinsel.
4. This next step is extremely important to achieve a smooth tinsel body: when tying in the tinsel, do one wrap to hold it in place, then wrap 6 more times towards the bend of the hook.
5. Once done, start wrapping the thread forward towards the eye with very close wraps, remembering to leave space for the head portion of the fly. When starting to wrap the tinsel, it will turn 180 degrees and then it will wrap flat. Lay one wrap of tinsel to the next, do not overlap, and stop once the thread is reached. Tie off the tinsel and trim.
6. Tie in two strands of peacock herl, then advance the thread to the eye and wrap the herl.
7. Tie off the herl, form the head, and whip finish. The fly is complete.

STU'S TIPS I must confess: I do not use strike indicators when fishing midges. It's just the way I was introduced to fishing chironomids. I will usually use this fly on still waters and do extremely well with it. Look for a submerged weed bed that is approximately 10 ft (3 m) deep and fish over that. I can't tell you how many big rainbows I've taken with that method. It's awesome!

NOTE Since I am a production tyer, I will do three to four dozen tinsel bodies, then head cement them four to five times, followed by the herl heads.

CB MIDGE BLACK

MATERIALS
Designed by Stu Thompson

Thread: Semperfli Nano Silk, 3/0, black

Hook: Daiichi 1120, size 8-18

Tail: Antron fibres, white

Body: Nano Silk, 3/0, black

Bead: Clear glass bead with a silver insert

1. De-barb the hook and slide the bead right behind the eye.
2. Place the hook in the vice and start the thread right behind the bead and do 7 or 8 wraps of thread.
3. Take a few fibres of white Antron and tie in right behind the bead, next wrap the thread in close wraps to the end of the shank of the hook. Bring the thread back towards the bead.
4. Start to form a nicely tapered body with the thread, butting the thread right to the bead.
5. Whip finish and the fly is just about complete.
6. Place the fly into a piece of foam and head cement the whole body. I usually apply 5 coats to each fly, waiting for the head cement to dry before another coat goes on. It is easier tying 3 or 4 dozen of these flies and then placing all of them on foam, then applying the head cement.

STU'S TIPS Fishing this fly is the same as fishing all other midge patterns but not only for trout. Lake whitefish, goldeye, mooneye, and tullibee (aka lake ciscoes) have been taken with this pattern. When fishing in rivers I always look for back eddies, no matter what size they are, and drift the fly throughout the eddy. If the fish are holding there, they just can't pass up this fly.

CB MIDGE WIRE

MATERIALS — *Designed by Stu Thompson*

Thread: Semperfli Nano Silk, 6/0, black

Hook: Daiichi 1120, size 8-14

Tail: Antron fibres, white

Body: Wire, fine, copper and green

Head: Peacock herl

Bead: Clear glass bead with silver insert

1. Slide the bead onto the hook and push it to the eye of the hook.
2. Place the hook in the vice and start the thread right behind the bead.
3. Tie in the Antron fibres for the tail and, in touching wraps, wrap the thread to the halfway point in the bend of the hook.
4. Tie in the wire, making sure the tag end reaches behind the bead, and wrap the thread back to the bead in touching wraps.
5. Advance the thread back to the rear of the bead, in touching wraps, leaving 1/16 in (1.5 mm) for the herl.
6. Wrap the copper and green wire to the point where the thread is and tie off.
7. Tie in a piece of peacock herl, wrap approximately 5 to 6 times, and tie it off.
8. Form a small head behind the bead and whip finish. The fly is complete.

STU'S TIPS I started tying this fly to get a chironomid pattern to sink a little faster. I didn't realize how well this fly works until I started to use it. Wow, am I ever glad I did! This pattern not only works in lakes, but it is just as effective on rivers. I was fishing the Assiniboine River (a secret spot) one afternoon and the carp were feeding like crazy. I couldn't see what they were feeding on, so I tied this pattern on. My first cast and, *whump!* The carp hit and took off like a freight train. What a fight; landed a 33-inch (83.8-cm) on a size 12 CB Midge Wire. Other fish caught on this fly: trout, sauger, perch, ciscoes, white bass, and suckers (most notably quillback).

RED BEAD MIDGE

MATERIALS
Designed by Stu Thompson

Thread: Semperfli Nano Silk, 3/0, red

Hook: Daiichi 1120, size 10-16

Body: Red beads

1. De-barb the hook and then place the beads into position.
2. Place the hook in the vice and tilt the hook forward.
3. Start the thread at the back of the hook, building up a base that the beads will not slip over and they will tighten up against one another.
4. Whip finish and the fly is complete.

STU'S TIPS There are many tyers who have designed a fly like this and I can't find any information on who developed this style of fly. This is one of the most interesting patterns to fish because the sink rate is a little faster than the traditional midge pattern. When fishing in still water, I use the one-and-a-half rule, which is if I want to fish at a 10-ft depth (3-m) I will use a leader that is 15 ft (4.57 m). This will ensure that the fly is at the proper depth and can be fished accordingly. I have taken quite a few different species on the pattern including goldeye, mooneye, sauger, walleye, and all the trout species.

NYMPHS

16	REBECCA'S DAMSEL		32	FFA CADDIS EMERGER
17	DARKWATER DAMSEL		33	MANITOBA MAYFLY
18	'52 BUICK		34	CHEATER'S CADDIS
19	JEN DRAGON		36	FFA STONEFLY
20	BODACIOUS DRAGON FLY NYMPH		38	DERRICK'S DEMON STONE
22	HUFF 'N FLUFF DRAGON		40	CORRIGAN'S CRAW
23	DARKWATER SWIMMER		43	THE MUNCHER
24	NIXON'S NYMPH		45	CALLI NYMPH
25	STU'S BACKSWIMMER		47	STU'S SOW BUG
26	FLOATING BACKSWIMMER		48	THE TICK
28	ABBOTT'S COSTELLO		50	BECK'S HEX
29	OWEN'S GOLDEN RETRIEVER			
30	ELASTIC BAND CADDIS			

 Easy
 Moderate
 Difficult

NYMPHS

These aquatic insects live in the water year round and provide fish with a consistent food source. No matter what kind of nymph it is, fish will feed on them.

Nick Laferriere with a fantastic pothole lake rainbow from the west side of Manitoba

Photo courtesy Nick Laferriere

REBECCA'S DAMSEL

MATERIALS

Designed by Stu Thompson

Thread: Semperfli Nano Silk, 6/0 black

Hook: Daiichi 1710, size 8-14

Tail: Tuft of Darkwater Dubbing, red olive

Body: Darkwater Dubbing, red olive

Eyes: Black shadow or black plastic bead chain

1. Place the hook in the vice and start the thread at the eye of the hook.
2. Tie in the eyes with figure eight wraps.
3. Wrap the thread along the shank just to the point of the barb.
4. Tie in a tail of Darkwater Dubbing material, then apply dubbing to the thread.
5. Form the body, stopping at the eyes.
6. Apply more dubbing to the thread and do figure-eight wraps around the eyes. Continue to build the dubbing to form the thorax of the fly.
7. Whip finish and the fly is complete.

STU'S TIPS Rebecca's Damsel was developed to give the fly tyer a pattern that would not take long to tie. The silhouette is the most important aspect and then the colour of the naturals in the body of water you are fishing. I have used this fly to also imitate several species of Mayfly nymphs with equal success. It can be tied in virtually any colour and it will work. Tans, olives, browns and blacks have all been successful colours. This pattern has taken crappie, bluegill, sauger, Rainbows, Brook, and Brown trout, as well as channel cats.

DARKWATER DAMSEL

MATERIALS
Designed by Stu Thompson

Thread: Semperfli Nano Silk, 6/0 black
Hook: Daiichi 1260, size 8-14
Tail: Darkwater Dubbing, olive
Body: Darkwater Dubbing, olive
Wing case: Scud back, amber
Eyes: Black plastic bead chain

1. Place the hook in the vice and start the thread at the eye of the hook.
2. Tie on the eyes near the eye of the hook with figure-eight wraps.
3. Wrap the thread towards the rear of the hook to the point of the barb.
4. Tie in the tail of Darkwater Dubbing (tyer's choice of colour).
5. Tie in the amber scud back.
6. Apply some Darkwater Dubbing to form the first quarter of the body.
7. Bring the scud back over it to form a wing case. Secure the scud back with wraps of thread, wrapping forward approximately 1/16 in (1.5 mm).
8. Fold the scud back and tie it down right in front of the first segment you made.
9. Apply some Darkwater Dubbing to form the second segment of the body. Repeat this step until you form segments reaching the eyes.
10. To form the thorax, repeat the previous step, but build the dubbing to form a thicker thorax.
11. Bring the scud back over, tie off, then whip finish.

STU'S TIPS This is one of a very few patterns that has been produced exclusively for trout. Numerous browns, rainbows, brook, and tigers have been caught using this fly. This pattern works well along a weed edge that is adjacent to a drop off. I have fished this fly down to 15 ft (4 m) and have had great success.

'52 BUICK

MATERIALS

Designed unknown, tied by Stu Thompson

Thread: Semperfli Nano Silk, 6/0, black

Hook: Daiichi 1710, size 8-14

Tail: Mallard breast feather fibres, natural or lemon

Body: Darkwater Dubbing, tan

Rib: Gold tinsel, medium oval

Throat: Mallard breast feather fibres, natural or lemon

Head: Peacock herl

1. Place the hook in the vice and start the thread behind the eye of the hook; wrap back to the point of the barb.
2. Tie in a tail of mallard breast feather fibres equal to three-quarters the length of the shank.
3. After securing the tail fibres, wrap the thread back to the point of the barb.
4. Tie in the ribbing material.
5. Dub the body, in this instance with tan Darkwater Dubbing, to within 1/8 in (3.2 mm) from the eye of the hook.
6. Advance the ribbing to the tie off point at the end of the dubbed body.
7. Invert the hook in the vice and tie in a throat of mallard fibres.
8. Then turn the hook right-side up and tie in the peacock herl. Wrap the peacock herl 3 to 4 times, then tie off, and whip finish.

STU'S TIPS This Alberta pattern has taken trout all across Canada and throughout the US. It is still one of the best trout-producing flies that has ever been tied and it's not too bad catching smallmouth, sauger, and white bass. I have tied this fly in olive, brown, and black as well as the above colour and no matter what colour I use, it catches fish.

JEN DRAGON

MATERIALS

Designed by Stu Thompson

Thread: Semperfli Nano Silk, 3/0, black

Hook: Daiichi 1260, size 6-14

Tail: Tuft of Darkwater Dubbing, dark olive

Underbody: Wool, black

Body: Darkwater Dubbing, dark olive

Wing case: Anti-static bag

Rib: Fine copper wire

Legs: Darkwater Dubbing, dark olive

Head: Darkwater Dubbing, dark olive

Eyes: Plastic bead chain, black rainbow or black

1. Place the hook in the vice and start the thread at the eye of the hook and wrap back to the point of the barb.
2. Tie in a tuft of Darkwater Dubbing, and ensure the thread is back at the point of the barb.
3. Tie in the copper wire, a piece of anti-static bag (for the wing case), and the black wool.
4. Wrap the black wool to form the under body along two-thirds of the shank and tie off.
5. Wrap the thread back to the point of the barb and dub the body over the black wool.
6. After the body is complete bring the anti-static bag over the body and secure it.
7. Wrap the copper wire in evenly spaced wraps to where you secured the wing case and tie off.
8. Tie in the eyes halfway between the eye of the hook and the finished abdomen.
9. Tie in another piece of anti-static bag so that it extends over the hook eye.
10. Make a dubbing loop, then place the dubbing crosswise in the loop, and spin it tight.
11. Wrap the loop twice in front of the abdomen and then do a figure eight around the eyes. Do one wrap in front of the eyes and another wrap behind the eyes: this is the tie off point.
12. Fold the bag back along the top of the hook, tie down, and whip finish.
13. With a pair of scissors, trim the hair away leaving enough for the legs.

STU'S TIPS In June, this fly just annihilates smallmouth and has taken various warm water species of fish. When fished correctly around weed beds it is unbeatable, if you find the right weed bed. What I look for is a weed bed that has an 8 ft (2.4 m) depth with openings in the middle of the bed. Casting to these open spots with this nymph is a blast because fish will just explode on this pattern.

BODACIOUS DRAGON FLY NYMPH

MATERIALS

Designed by Stu Thompson

Thread: Semperfli Nano Silk, 6/0, black

Hook: Daiichi 1720, size 8-14

Tail: Goose biots, brown

Underbody: Black wool

Body: Chenille, brown

Wing Case: Ultra chenille, brown

Thorax: Darkwater Dubbing, dark tan

Eyes: Black bead chain

1. Place the hook in the vice and start the thread at the eye of the hook.
2. Tie in the eyes with a figure eight wrap.
3. Wrap the thread to the point of the barb.
4. Tie in 3 goose biots—one on each side and one on top of the hook shank.
5. Tie in the brown chenille, then wrap the thread to the rear of the eyes.
6. Tie in the black wool, form the abdomen, then tie off.
7. Wrap the chenille to the rear of the eyes and tie it off, securing with another half a dozen wraps.
8. Cut a piece of ultra chenille long enough to form the head of the thorax and the wing case.
9. Singe both ends of the ultra chenille with a flame (candles work best).
10. Double the ultra chenille and lay it between the eyes and secure with a figure eight wrap. At this point, the burned ends of the chenille will be past the eye of the hook.
11. Let out approximately 3 in (7.6 cm) of thread and apply the dubbing to make a noodle.
12. Wrap around the eyes, then do 1 wrap in front of the eyes and 2 wraps behind the eyes.
13. Tie off the dubbing noodle behind the eyes.
14. Fold the chenille over the eyes and tie down.
15. After securing the chenille, whip finish and the fly is complete.

STU'S TIPS One of my tried and true methods of fishing this nymph may surprise a few people. I usually wait until 9:30 p.m. and crawl this pattern along a sandy bottom on the edge of marl weeds, in about 8 ft (2.5 m) of water. Trout will always cruise this area at dusk and will eagerly take the fly.

One heck of a fight and one I will never forget.

BELIEVE IT OR not, this is a sturgeon on the fly—absolutely true. I was actually drifting my fly along the edge of a hole, hoping for a channel cat. I felt a light tap on the fly and set the hook. When I first started to fight this sturgeon, I didn't know what type of fish it was. Cats usually have a back and forth motion, carp are a dead straight away run, and drum are head shakers. This fish didn't do anything like that. In fact, it took off like a Polaris missile, jumping straight up in the air trying to get rid of the brown DDH Leech it had engulfed. One heck of a fight and one I will never forget. My first sturgeon on the fly and it was a riot. The Red River has never let me down.

HUFF 'N FLUFF DRAGON

MATERIALS

Designed by Stu Thompson

Thread: Semperfli Nano Silk, 6/0, black

Hook: Daiichi 1710, size 8-14

Tail: Mallard breast feather fibres

Body: Darkwater Dubbing, red olive

Throat: Mallard breast feather fibres

Head: Peacock herl

1. Place the hook in the vice and start the thread behind the hook eye and wrap back to the point of the barb.
2. Tie in the mallard fibres for a tail, securing the fibres down.
3. Form a dubbing loop (please see page 188 for instructions). Place dubbing mixture crosswise between the two threads and twist tight.
4. Brush out any loose fibres with a small battery brush or Velcro brush.
5. Wrap the dubbing towards the eye of the hook, stopping approximately 1/8 in (3 mm) from the eye, then tying off.
6. Invert the hook and tie in a throat of mallard fibres.
7. Turn the hook right-side up and tie in 3 strands of peacock herl. Complete 2 to 3 wraps, then tie this off and whip finish.
8. Once complete, take the battery or Velcro brush and brush out any trapped dubbing and the fly is finished.

STU'S TIPS The similarity of this fly to a '52 Buick is understandable since I wanted to see what type of fly I could come up with when I "DDHd" a typical nymph. As you can see, it turned out not too badly and has been a consistent fly for producing trout. I have also taken smallmouth with this pattern, but I have yet to try it on other species.

DARKWATER SWIMMER

MATERIALS

Designed by Stu Thompson

Thread: Semperfli Nano Silk 6/0, white (colour with an olive felt marker)

Hook: Daiichi 1550, size 8-16

Tail: None

Wing Case: Summer Duck scud, back

Body: Darkwater Dubbing, olive

Legs: Barred brown or black rubber legs

1. Place the hook in the vice and start the thread behind the hook eye, wrapping towards the back of the hook to the point of the barb.
2. Tie in the scud back wing case and secure the tag end.
3. Advance the thread approximately half way up the shank, then tie in the rubber legs and secure with figure-eight wraps.
4. Wrap back to the point of the barb and apply dubbing to the thread.
5. Advance the newly formed dubbing noodle towards the eye of the hook, but remember to figure eight around the legs.
6. The dubbing should be wrapped to the eye of the hook.
7. Bring the scud back over the body and secure it, then trim the excess. Form the head and whip finish.

STU'S TIPS This fly was designed for some of the still water fisheries that abound on the west side of my home province of Manitoba. The fish here typically have a growth rate of 2.5 lbs (1 kg) per year. During the spring, backswimmers and water boatmen are the first insects to become active and are actively pursued by trout. In the fall, their mating flights will bring out some of the biggest trout as they gorge themselves on this insect.

23

NIXON'S NYMPH

MATERIALS

Designed by Stu Thompson

Thread: Semperfli Nano Silk, 6/0, black
Hook: Daiichi 1530, size 8-16
Body: Peacock herl
Wing Case: Peacock herl
Legs: Peacock herl

1. Place the hook in the vice and start the thread at the eye of the hook.
2. Wrap the thread back to the point of the barb.
3. Take approximately 20 strands of peacock herl and tie them in. The herl has to go to the eye of the hook.
4. Take 5 or 6 strands of herl, wrap them forward, and tie off at the eye.
5. Fold the rest of the herl over the body and tie down at the eye.
6. Pick up 2 strands of herl, one on each side, and tie them back so the tips of the herl are past the bend of the hook.
7. After securing the rest of the herl at the eye, trim the tag ends.
8. Form the head and whip finish.
9. Hold the two long pieces of herl that go past the bend and trim with the scissors. Make sure the length of the legs equals the bend of the hook.

STU'S TIPS This easy to tie pattern is actually one of the first flies I started tying. I'm still using it some 55 years later, and it still catches trout like crazy. Twice a year, I really concentrate on using this fly. The first is when the ice is just off the water—these insects are the first active ones of the year and fish just can't resist them. The second time I use this fly is when the mating flight occurs in fall. Late September to early October will usually have the backswimmers and boatman very active. If you time it right, you can have a day of fishing beyond belief. The right place *and* right time with this fly? You could have a 150-fish day.

STU'S BACKSWIMMER

MATERIALS

Designed by Stu Thompson

Thread: Semperfli Nano Silk 6/0 black

Hook: Daiichi 1550, size 10-16

Wing Case: Peacock herl

Body: Darkwater Dubbing, tan

1. Place the hook in the vice and start the thread behind the eye of the hook. Wrap back to the point of the barb.
2. Take 10 to 12 strands of peacock herl and tie them in on top of the hook shank. Leave the butt ends of the herl long enough to form an underbody.
3. Once the underbody is secure, wrap the thread back to the point of the barb.
4. Let out approximately 3 inches (7.6 cm.) and apply the dubbing with a one directional spinning motion. Wrap the newly formed dubbing noodle forward to the eye of the hook stopping 1/16 in. (1.5 mm) from the eye.
5. Bring the peacock herl over the dubbed body and secure it at the eye of the hook with 4 or 5 wraps of thread.
6. Take one strand of herl from each side and fold them back along the side of the body to form the legs. Secure these two pieces down with 4 or 5 wraps of thread.
7. Trim off the excess herl at the hook eye, form the head, and whip finish.
8. Trim the legs - the two pieces that you tied back earlier - so the length reaches the bend of the hook. The fly is now complete and ready for head cement.

STU'S TIPS I needed a pattern that would work and which I could tie in a hurry. The above result is that fly. In a pinch, I can tie 18 of these flies in just over an hour. Do they work? You bet! It is one of the best patterns to use in early spring or late fall and can't be beat for trout to 30 inches (76.2 cm) and smallmouth to 20 in. (50.8 cm). It's the insect that will tell you where they are located during autumn. When you see a mass of black bugs flying around the surface of the water in late September or early October, you know to tie on one of these flies. The fishing is fast and furious.

FLOATING BACKSWIMMER

MATERIALS

Designed by Stu Thompson

Thread: Semperfli Nano Silk 3/0, black

Hook: Daiichi 1550, size 4-14

Bottom wing case: White 5/64 in (2 mm) foam

Top wing case: Black 5/64 in (2 mm) foam

Legs: Round rubber, brown

1. Place the hook in the vice and start the thread behind the hook eye, wrapping towards the point of the barb.

2. Invert the hook in the vice and tie in the bottom wing case of white foam, securing the foam by wrapping the thread towards the eye of the hook.

3. Turn the hook right side up in the vice and tie in the black foam as in the previous step.

4. At this point, the thread should be approximately 1/16 inch (1.5 mm) from the eye. Wrap the thread towards the bend of the hook, stopping about one-third of the way down the hook shank.

5. Tie in the round rubber hackle legs with figure-eight wraps and wrap the thread back towards the eye.

6. Bring the white foam to the eye of the hook and tie it down, then repeat this step for the black foam.

7. Secure both pieces of foam with 10 wraps of thread and whip finish. Trim the foam close to the eye.

STU'S TIPS The #4, #6, and # 8 sizes of this fly will effectively imitate the predaceous diving beetles that mate in the fall. The smaller sizes will imitate boatman and backswimmers during their mating flight. This pattern is best fished in the fall when these insects are most active.

BONUS FLY

A hefty smallmouth that inhaled a tan DDH minnow, caught on the east side of Manitoba.

ABBOTT'S COSTELLO

MATERIALS

Designed by Stu Thompson

Thread: Monocord 3/0, black
Hook: Mustad 37160, size 2-10
Body: Ultra chenille, chartreuse
Head: Darkwater Dubbing, black and chartreuse

1. Place the hook in the vice and start the thread at the eye of the hook.
2. Wrap the thread one-quarter of the way back to the bend of the hook.
3. Tie in the chartreuse ultra-chenille and continue to wrap the thread until you reach the half way point of the bend.
4. Wrap the thread forward three-quarters of the way back to the hook eye.
5. Wrap the chenille to form a tapered body.
6. Tie off the chenille and form a dubbing loop.
7. Place the Darkwater Dubbing crosswise in the loop and spin tight.
8. Finally, wrap the dubbing loop to form the head and tie off. Add head cement and the fly is finished.

STU'S TIPS This pattern is a killer at times, especially when the caddis are moving. The carp seem to love this colour combination and it is one of my go-to flies when carp are being difficult. I have always fished this pattern when I see tailing carp. This fly, tied in smaller sizes, will fish well for walleye or trout in rivers. Although designed for carp, this fly has taken 10 different species of fish.

OWEN'S GOLDEN RETRIEVER

MATERIALS — *Designed and tied by Ken Sawich*

Thread: Semperfli Nano Silk, 6/0, black

Hook: Daiichi 1710, size 6 or 8

Tail: Pheasant tail church window soft hackle

Body: Soft underfur from a golden retriever (in this case, Ken's dog)

Bead: 1/8 in (3 mm) gold bead

1. De-barb the hook and slide the gold bead on.
2. Place the hook in the vice and start the thread right behind the bead. Wrap the thread to the point of the barb.
3. Select 3 or 4 fibres from the pheasant church window feather and tie in as a tail.
4. Let out approximately 4 in (10 cm) of thread and apply the dubbing to make a noodle.
5. Place the dubbing twister in the middle of the thread and fold it back towards the hook shank.
6. Wrap the thread around the shank securing the dubbing loop.
7. Twist tight and wrap the loop towards the back of the bead.
8. Once at the back of the bead, tie off the noodle, form a head, and whip finish. The fly is complete.

NOTE: Pheasant tail church window soft hackle feathers, which have brown edges and a white centre, are located by the rump feathers on the bird.

KEN'S FISHING LOG "The first time I fished this fly, I had terrific success with it. I decided to try out my luck on the shores of Lake Manitoba after my brother-in-law, Lorman, told me about the carp feeding in the shallows. I tried a couple of different patterns to no avail and then I remembered the fly I just tied out of my dog's fur. After 3 or 4 casts, I had a hit, set the hook and proceeded to have the fight of my life. After 7 or 8 runs and 15 minutes fighting, this fish I finally landed a 32-in (0.8 m) behemoth of a carp. What a fish! Believe it or not, the next cast brought its cousin to net as well. Another 32-incher! I decided not to ruin my good fortune, so I took a well-needed rest. What an adrenalin rush. Fly fishing carp, cats, or freshwater drum—this is one fly that is hard to beat."

Well, said Ken. I know I'll be using this fly.

ELASTIC BAND CADDIS

MATERIALS

Designed by Stu Thompson

Thread: Semperfli Nano Silk, 6/0, white (use an olive felt marker to color the whiite thread)

Hook: Daiichi 1710, size 8-14

Tail: None

Body: Elastic band, tan

Head: Peacock herl

1. Place the hook in the vice and start the thread right behind the eye of the hook.
2. Wrap the thread back to the point of the barb in very close and tight wraps so the whole of the shank is covered in a layer of thread.
3. Tie in the elastic band and leave a tag end that is 1/16 inch (1.5 mm) long. The reason for doing this is when the thread is wrapped forward in close wraps towards the eye of the hook, the elastic band tag end will squeeze out towards the eye of the hook, keeping a uniform body diameter throughout the fly.
4. Wrap the elastic band towards the eye of the hook, keeping enough tension on it to make the colour change from tan to white. When tying off the elastic band, wrap the thread 10 to 15 times at the tie off point to secure the band. If you don't do this step properly, the elastic will slip from the tie-off point when you stretch it to cut it off.
5. After tying off the elastic band, add 2 or 3 strands of peacock herl and secure it into place.
6. Advance the thread to the eye of the hook, then wrap the herl to form the head of the fly.
7. Tie the herl off and form a small thread head. Whip finish and the fly is complete.

STU'S TIPS It's amazing what a 15-year-old mind can conjure up when playing with an elastic band. The first time I used this fly, I caught eight trout on eight casts. Believe it or not, I still use this same fly 50 years later. It is one of the best free-swimming caddis patterns I have devised. Another note on this fly: if you want to change the colour a bit, you can use a Pantone marker or just use a different colour of elastic band.

Stephen Jay with a typical freshwater drum.

FFA CADDIS EMERGER

MATERIALS

Designed by Stu Thompson

Thread: Semperfli Nano Silk, 6/0, white (colour with an olive felt marker)

Hook: Mustad 37160, size 10-14

Tail: Pheasant rump fibres, green

Body: Seal fur or substitute, cream

Rib: Seal fur or substitute, olive

Antennae: Fibres from a pheasant tail

Wing pad: Pheasant rump, green

Head: After shaft philoplume from the inside of a pheasant rump feather

1. Place the hook in the vice and start the thread at the eye of the hook, then wrap to the barb.
2. Tie in some green pheasant rump fibres for a tail.
3. Take some olive seal fur dubbing (or substitute) and create a dubbing noodle that is twice as long as you need it.
4. Fold the dubbing in half with a dubbing twister and place out of the way. Don't forget to do a half hitch at this point.
5. Apply some cream seal fur to the thread for another dubbing noodle, which once again will be doubled and twisted tight.
6. Advance the thread towards the eye of the hook and do another half hitch.
7. Twist the cream dubbing tight and advance it forward, stopping once three-quarters of the hook shank is covered and tie it off.
8. Next, take the olive dubbing noodle and twist it tight. Once tightened, wrap this material as a rib on the body and tie it off at the same spot as the cream dubbing.
9. For the wing pad, tie in another green pheasant rump feather and wrap this 2 to 3 times in the same place and tie off.
10. Push the fibres down and secure the feather by wrapping around it to form the wing pad.
11. Then take two centre pheasant tail fibres and tie one on each side for the antennae.
12. Use a pheasant philoplume (found on the inside of a rump feather) for the head portion of the fly. Tie it in and wrap it forward. A word of caution: do not use excessive force with the philoplume because they are a fragile feather and break easily.
13. Form the head and tie off.

STU'S TIPS This fly has taken 11 different species of fish and when the caddis are hatching it is a deadly representation of the living insect. Using a dry line and fishing this fly a couple of inches underneath the surface of the water is deadly.

MANITOBA MAYFLY

MATERIALS

Designed by Stu Thompson

Thread: Semperfli Nano Silk, 6/0 white (colour it olive with a felt marker)

Hook: Daiichi 1720, size 14-8

Tail: Hackle fibres, dun

Abdomen: Darkwater Dubbing (colour is tyer's choice)

Wing case: Turkey quill, mottled brown

Legs: Hackle, dun

Thorax: Darkwater Dubbing (colour is tyer's choice)

1. Place the hook in the vice, start the thread at the eye of the hook and wrap back to the point of the barb.
2. Select the dun hackle fibres by stripping them off the quill. The tail should equal the length of half the shank of the hook.
3. Once done, dub some Darkwater Dubbing and create a tapered abdomen.
4. Tie in the wing case of turkey quill and then tie in a dun hackle for the legs.
5. Let out approximately 3 in (7.5 cm) of thread and apply some Darkwater Dubbing by twisting the dubbing in one direction.
6. Wrap the newly formed dubbing noodle to build the thorax. Palmer the hackle through the thorax 2 to 3 times and tie off.
7. Fold the wing case over the thorax and tie down.
8. Complete the fly by head cementing.

STU'S TIPS Dead drifting this nymph in rivers is deadly, especially when the brown drake mayflies start to hatch. I have had tremendous success with multiple species on this pattern. It can also be tied in a light tan colour to imitate the *Hexagenia limbata* hatch which occurs in Manitoba. This fly also works in still water situations and many a trout have fallen prey to it in both colours.

CHEATER'S CADDIS

MATERIALS

Designed by Stu Thompson

Thread: Semperfli Nano Silk, 6/0, white (colour with an olive felt marker)

Hook: Mustad 37160, size 10-14

Underbody: 5/64 in (2 mm) foam, yellow

Tail: Pheasant rump fibers, green

Body: Summer duck scud, back

Wing pad: Pheasant rump

Antennae: Pheasant tail fibres

Head: Darkwater Dubbing, brown

1. Place the hook in the vice and start the thread at the eye of the hook.
2. Wrap the thread to the halfway point of the bend.
3. Tie in the tail of pheasant rump and secure with thread wraps (approximately halfway down on the hook bend).
4. Tie in the scud back and secure with thread wraps.
5. Tie in the yellow foam, then advance the thread three-quarters up the hook shank.
6. Wrap the foam to the thread and tie it off, securing it.
7. Wrap the scud back over the foam to complete the body. Ensure you tie off at the same point as the foam.
8. Tie in the pheasant rump as the wing pad by wrapping the hackle around the hook shank, then force all the fibres underneath the hook shank, and secure with the thread.
9. For antennae, tie in one pheasant tail fibre on each side and secure.
10. Form a dubbing loop by letting out approximately 5 in (12.5 cm) of thread.
11. Place the dubbing twister in the middle and fold the thread back to the hook shank. Secure the loop with 5 wraps of thread.
12. Place dubbing mixture crosswise into the loop and twist tight.
13. Brush out any loose fibres with a small battery brush or a Velcro brush.
14. Wrap the dubbing noodle to form the head and tie off.
15. Form the thread head and tie off.

STU'S TIPS This pattern is a favourite of mine and I have used it for catching walleye, sauger, white bass, smallmouth, goldeye, mooneye, lake whitefish, carp, rainbows, browns, brookies, and even the occasional channel cat. The foam in this fly will make it float just underneath the surface film and the fish simply can't resist a well presented fly. Checking my log, my best night of fishing this pattern was 47 fish.

Stephen Jay tying one on at Lockport, Manitoba, while fishing on the Red River

FFA STONEFLY

MATERIALS

Designed by Stu Thompson

Thread: Monocord, 3/0, tan

Hook: Mustad 33665A, size 6

Butt: Golden angora goat

Tail: Hackle stems, brown

Abdomen underbody: 4 strips of lead wire

Abdomen: Golden angora goat

Wing case: Turkey quill, brown

First thorax: Angora goat dubbing

Second thorax: Grizzly hackle and angora goat

1. Bend one-quarter of the front of the 3665A hook to a 30-degree angle.
2. Place the hook in the vice and start the thread at the bend you just made.
3. Cut four pieces of lead wire to equal the length of the straight hook shank. Tie one piece along the side of the hook shank and repeat the process for the other side.
4. Tie in the third piece along the side of the first piece of lead wire and repeat for the other side. Wrap the thread to the back of the hook.
5. Take a pair of smooth-edge pliers and squeeze the lead wire flat. This will give the proper proportions of the abdomen of the nymph.
6. Dub some cream angora goat onto the thread with a one directional spinning motion of your thumb and index finger. Wrap the very back of the hook to form a small butt section.
7. Strip two brown hackle feathers to use for the tail. Tie in one on each side. The length of the tail is 1.5 times the length of the abdomen.
8. Form a dubbing loop by letting out approximately 6 in (15.24 cm) of thread. Place the dubbing twister in the middle of the thread and fold it back up to the hook shank. To secure the loop, do 5 to 6 turns of thread then advance the thread to the bend you created in the hook.
9. Place the angora goat crosswise in the loop and spin tight. Wrap this noodle to the thread and tie off. Whip finish and trim the thread.
10. Take the fly out of the vice and trim the hair as close as possible, making sure you don't cut the tail.
11. Place the hook back into the vice and start the thread again.
12. Cut a section of turkey quill the same width as the body, and tie it in on top of the hook shank.
13. After the quill is secure, form another dubbing loop, place the angora goat crosswise in the loop, and spin tight. Take a small battery brush or Velcro brush and brush out the loose fibres
14. Wrap the noodle halfway down the bent portion of the hook and tie off.
15. Fold the first wing case over. Use your scissors to make the straight edge of the wing case by placing the inside edge against the quill and folding it over the scissors. Pull out the scissors and hold the quill down, then do 2 or 3 wraps to hold it into place. Trim the excess and secure.
16. Tie in the second wing case and secure. The width of this wing case is three-quarters the size of the first one.
17. Tie in a grizzly hackle so the feather is curving away from you.

A goldeye that wanted to munch on a DDH Eyes White Minnow. These fish will hit with reckless abandon.

18. Form another dubbing loop, place the angora goat crosswise in the loop, and spin tight. Brush out any loose fibres with a battery or Velcro brush.
19. Wrap the dubbing noodle to cover the rest of the shank, remembering to leave enough room for the head.
20. Wrap the grizzly hackle through the second thorax 2 to 3 times, then tie off.
21. Fold the second wing case over, following the previous procedure for the first wing case.
22. Form a thread head and whip finish.

STU'S TIPS When fishing this fly for trout, try the riffle water since stoneflies like highly oxygenated water. When fishing walleye, cast along the current seams close to the shoreline. When the stoneflies hatch they will climb out of the water, usually among the rocks, then wait for the sun to dry and split their skin. This migration always triggers a feeding frenzy for walleye.

DEREK'S DEMON STONE

MATERIALS

Designed by Stu Thompson

Thread: Semperfli Nano Silk, 6/0, black

Hook: Daiichi 1730, size 4-10

Butt: Darkwater Dubbing, black

Tail: Black goose biots

Underbody: Lead wire 0.03

Body: Rayon chenille, black

Legs: Goose biots, black

Thorax: Seal dun angora

Wing case: Black turkey quill (coated with two coats of head cement)

1. Select a black turkey quill feather and use head cement to coat it. Let it dry overnight, then apply a second coat and let that dry overnight. (As a production tyer, I will take the time to do this because it saves quite a bit of time when tying this fly.)
2. Place the hook in the vice, start the thread at the eye of the hook, and wrap back to the bend.
3. Cut four strips of lead wire long enough to measure three-quarters of the hook shank.
4. Tie in the first strip along the side of the hook shank; repeat for the other side.
5. Place the second strip along the side of the first strip and secure. Repeat this step for the other side.
6. Cover the lead strips with thread and ensure all the lead wire is covered.
7. Take a pair of smooth-edge pliers and squeeze the lead flat so that it increases the width of the shank.
8. Apply a small amount of black dubbing to the thread and form the butt of the fly.
9. Tie in two black goose biots (one on each side) and secure with the thread.
10. Tie in the black chenille and wrap it forward until reaching the bend in the shank of the hook.
11. Tie off the chenille and secure.
12. Cut a segment of turkey quill equal to the width of the body and tie in on top of the hook shank.
13. Tie in the black goose biots for legs (one on each side).
14. Form a dubbing loop, place the seal dun dubbing crosswise in the loop, and spin tight.
15. Brush out the loose fibres with a small battery brush or Velcro brush.
16. Do two complete wraps and then tie off the loop.
17. Fold over the first wing case by placing a flat edge of the scissors against the quill and then fold over.
18. Tie down the first wing case and secure.
19. Cut a narrower piece of turkey quill, three-quarters the width of the first one, and tie in on top of the hook shank.
20. Tie in the second set of goose biots (one on each side).
21. Repeat the dubbing loop process to finish the thorax.
22. Once again, fold the quill over using the same steps as the previous wing case.
23. Tie down the wing case and secure it. Add the last set of goose biot legs, one on each side, form the head and whip finish. Head cement the thread and the fly is complete.

Brown trout caught on an olive DDH Leech.

STU'S TIPS This fly was originally designed to imitate the Pteronarcys (giant stoneflies) that are found in the Bow River in Calgary, where I had the occasional opportunity to fish. I decided to do some investigating on the Winnipeg River in my home province and found an abundance of stoneflies living in this water. During the following years, this pattern has taken walleye, sauger, smallmouth bass, lake whitefish, and yellow perch.

Fishing this pattern is no different than fishing it for trout. Quartering the cast upstream and doing a dead drift will take all of the above species. The areas that are overlooked on a river are the foam patches that sometimes occur along the shoreline. Insects cannot get through the foam and, as a result get trapped, providing the fish a virtual smorgasbord of food items. I'll drop this fly in the middle of the foam patch and I am always rewarded with a pleasant surprise.

CORRIGAN'S CRAW

MATERIALS

Designed by Mike Corrigan

Thread: Semperfli Fluoro Brite, dark orange #5

Hook: Daiichi 1720, size 6

Tail: Zonker rabbit strip, brown; and 2–4 strands of Krystal Flash, pearl

Pinchers: Ultra chenille, small, red/brown, 5–6 in (13–15 cm) in length

Antenna: Hairbrush fibres (from a "Goody" hairbrush)

Legs: Barred red/brown rubber legs

Eyes: Bead chain or dumbbell, small to medium

Body: Antron, rust; and Darkwater Dubbing, brown

Rib: Copper wire, fine

1. Create the pinchers by knotting the ultra-chenille at the open end and then knotting the loop end, leaving a 1/4 in (7 to 8 mm) tag. Cut the loop in the middle: both ends should now look the same. Carefully singe the ends over a candle to seal the chenille.
2. Place the hook in the vice and start the thread at the eye of the hook.
3. Tie in the dumbbell or bead chain eyes in a figure eight wrap, leaving a 1/16 in (2 mm) gap near the eye of the hook. Add a drop of Krazy Glue to secure the eyes.
4. Wrap the thread to the point of the barb.
5. Pull out a pair of "eyes" from the "Goody" hairbrush with a pair of offset pliers. Tie in on top of the hook shank, just above the point of the barb. Tie in at the middle point of the pair of "eyes" and then rotate the stems so they are along the side of the hook shank. Continue wrapping the thread until the eyes are secure. Bend the fibres outward so that they form a 45-degree angle to one another. Add a drop of Krazy Glue to ensure they stay in place.
6. Apply a clump of marabou or rabbit fur the same length as the antennae on top of the hook shank.
7. Tie in the Krystal Flash; length is one to one-and-a-half times the hook shank length.
8. Tie in the pinchers so that they extend past the bend of the hook by one shank length.
9. Rotate the hook in the vice.
10. Tie in the Antron fibres that will form the back of the fly. The fibres will extend past the bend of the hook.
11. Apply the dubbing to the thread and start the newly formed noodle from the rear of the hook towards the eye. Stop approximately one-third of the way to the eye and tie in the rubber legs—3 on each side.
12. Once the legs are tied in, apply the wire for the rib. Continue to wrap the dubbing to form a nicely tapered body. Stop at the front of the eyes.
13. Pull the Antron over the hook towards the eye and tie off, leaving a 1/4 in (1 cm) overhang.
14. Wrap the copper wire 3 to 4 times over the Antron, towards the eye, making a segmented body. Tie off the copper wire.
15. Form the head and whip finish.
16. With a fine-tip felt marker, add black to the entire central portion of the Antron.

What a magnificent bone fish.
This is what dreams are made of.
Photo courtesy of Mike Corrigan

MIKE'S TIPS "Besides bass and trout, I have had several really good days on the Red River fishing for catfish. It can be a bit of a complicated tie, but it works well and looks great in the fly box."

What Mike doesn't know is that I have taken walleye, pike, and freshwater drum on this pattern as well. In my opinion, it is one fly that should be carried in every box.

A good-sized sauger caught on a Rebecca's Damsel.

THE MUNCHER

MATERIALS

Designed by Ian Colin James; tied by Stephen Jay

Thread: UNI-Thread, 8/0, black

Hook: Daiichi 1130, size 8-14

Abdomen: Darkwater Dubbing, tan (or tan yarn)

Rib: Red wire

Wing Cases: Swiss straw, brown

Legs: Hen feather, brown

Thorax: Darkwater Dubbing, brown

1. Place the hook in the vice and start the thread at the eye of the hook. Wrap the thread back to a quarter of the bend of the hook.
2. Tie in the wire for the rib and secure it with thread wraps.
3. Let approximately 5 in (13 cm) of thread out and apply the tan dubbing with a spinning motion of the thumb and index finger.
4. Advance the newly formed dubbing noodle approximately two-thirds up the hook shank and tie off.
5. Wrap the wire 4 to 5 times to make a segmented body.
6. Tie in the first wing case of Swiss straw.
7. Tie in a brown hen feather.
8. Create another dubbing noodle of brown dubbing.
9. Wrap half the distance to the eye of the hook with the dubbing noodle, then do two wraps of hackle and tie it off.
10. Bring the Swiss straw over and tie down. After the wing case is secure, fold it back towards the bend of the hook.
11. Tie in another hen hackle and repeat the previous process of doing the thorax.
12. Form the head and whip finish.

STEPHEN'S TIP "This pattern was originally tied by Ian Collin James of Grand River fame. It is, as many of my go-to patterns tend to be, an attractor style of fly. It doesn't imitate anything specifically; it merely has triggers that entice a strike from both salmonid and warm water species. When fishing, this is a great searching pattern for new waters. It will entice a strike from carp, freshwater drum, goldeye, and trout. It is supposed to be effective on still water as well; however, I have only ever fished it in rivers and creeks. As always try and get it near the bottom and do a very slow retrieve."

Gord Pyzer, of Outdoor Canada magazine, with his first freshwater drum on the fly. He was using an Erickson's Clouser in white, red, and black.

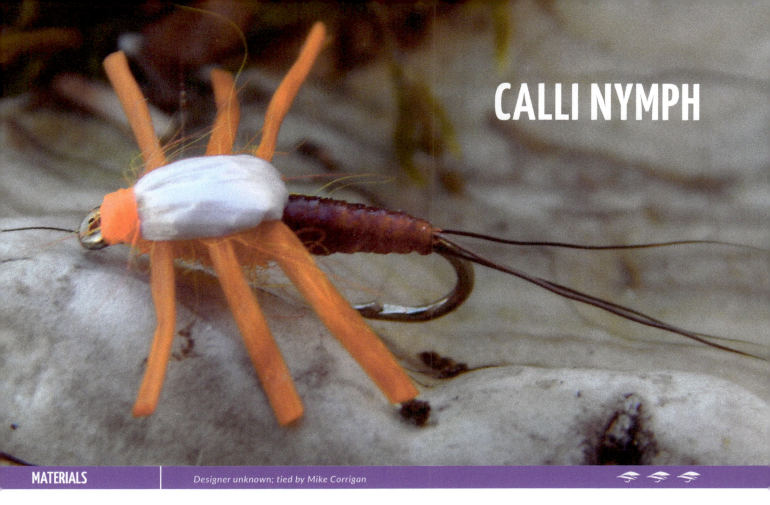

CALLI NYMPH

MATERIALS — *Designer unknown; tied by Mike Corrigan*

Thread: Semperfli Nano Silk, orange 12/0

Hook: Daiichi 1720, size 10-16

Tail: Moose body hair

Body: Summer Duck, scud back

Wing Case: Swiss straw, beige

Legs: Midge flex, amber

Thorax: Darkwater Dubbing, sunrise orange

1. Place the hook in the vice and start the thread at the eye of the hook. Wrap the thread back to the point of the barb.
2. Tie in three strands of moose body hair—one on top of the hook shank and one on each side of the hook.
3. Tie in the Summer Duck scud back.
4. With the thread make a nicely tapered body that will cover two-thirds of the hook shank.
5. Wrap the Summer Duck scud back once over the hair that is on top of the hook shank. When bringing the scud back around the hook shank, move the two hairs on each side of the hook out of the way.
6. With the next wrap of scud back, wrap the material around the two hairs that were missed with the first wrap.
7. Continue wrapping the scud back, tying off where the thread has stopped.
8. Tie in a wing case of Swiss straw.
9. Tie in three sets of legs on the thorax portion of the fly.
10. Let out approximately 3 in (7.5 cm) of thread and apply the dubbing by spinning it on the thread, creating a dubbing noodle.
11. Wrap the dubbing around onto the legs to get the first 2 pair angled backwards and the front pair angled forwards. Ensure the thread ends at the eye of the hook.
12. Pull the Swiss straw over and tie down.
13. Form the head and whip finish. The fly is complete.

STU'S STORY When the hatches start it is an amazing sight. Roughly 76 species hatch per year in my home province. The *Hexagenia limbata* probably has the biggest hatch, averaging 4.2 metric tonnes per year. But this pattern was not made for the larger mayflies; it is the smaller critters I was thinking of when this fly was given to me. I wish I could remember who it was because this fly in the cool evenings of August rises to the occasion so to speak. I have used this fly to take all manner of fish, with some of the most memorable being quillbacks and freshwater drum. Yes, two fish that you thought would never hit a mayfly nymph but will take this imitation with reckless abandon. Kudos for the person who tied it and gave it to me; you deserve the recognition. I just wish I could remember who it was.

My son, Kevin, with a Calli nymph quillback.

STU'S SOW BUG

MATERIALS

Designed by Stu Thompson

Thread: Semperfli Nano Silk, 6/0, white (colour with a brown felt marker)

Hook: Daiichi 1550, size 10-16

Underbody: Wool, olive

Body: Angora dubbing, cream (the back is coloured with a brown Pantone marker)

1. Place the hook in the vice. Tie in the olive wool and create a body that is built up in the middle.
2. Wrap the thread back to the bend of the hook and create a dubbing loop. Place the angora dubbing crosswise in the loop and spin tight.
3. Wrap the dubbing loop around the underbody, then tie it off.
4. Once completed, take the fly out of the vice and trim the dubbing quite short.
5. Take the brown marker and colour the top of the fly, remembering to let the ink dry completely. Head cement and the fly is finished.

STU'S TIP Fishing this fly in rivers follows all the rules; dead drift and mending are essential. I have also used this fly in still water situations, in which case I believe the fish will take it for a backswimmer or water boatman. Casting to weed edges in spring will bring resounding strikes.

THE TICK

MATERIALS

Designer unknown; tied by Stu Thompson

Thread: Semperfli Nano Silk, 6/0, black

Hook: Daiichi 1550, size 12-8

Body: Ostrich herl, grey

Wing case: Ostrich herl, grey

Hackle: Chinese rooster hackle, brown

1. Start the thread at the eye of the hook and wrap back to the point of the barb. Tie in 8-10 grey ostrich herls for a wing case.
2. Next, tie in the brown hackle and make sure it is secure. Take 4–5 ostrich herls for the body and tie them in by the butts. Advance the thread and wrap the herl to form the body.
3. Wrap the brown hackle in evenly spaced turns, advancing to the eye of the hook, then tie off.
4. Fold over the ostrich herl wing case and tie down, form the head, and tie off. A drop of head cement will finish the fly.

STU'S STORY This fly represents nothing and everything. It is a great imitation of something that looks alive in the water and will duplicate just about any aquatic insect that is found. The person who showed me this fly actually said that this was his best trout pellet imitation ever. It has been used on the rivers of Montana for native natural trout and on the stocked trout lakes of Manitoba's Parklands area with equal success. This fly can be fished at any depth using any retrieve. The best way to fish it is on a dry line with a 14 ft (4 m) leader. Fish it as slow as a chironomid, giving an extra little twitch every few feet. This style of fishing is deadly.

KEN SAWICH is an unassuming fly fisher, and is usually the one standing off to the side and watching what other fly fishermen are doing. He puts together the information, then out-catches everyone around him. He doesn't consider himself as a great fly designer, but I have to admit his patterns catch fish—and a lot of them. His Claret Tiger Leech is a trout or bass fly that you cannot do without, as you can see by the above picture. His Owen's Golden Retriever pattern has taken huge carp, with the best being 35 in (1 m). I had another friend use this fly in spring of 2020 while we were hunting carp in the shallows. Without a doubt, it out-fished every other fly I had tried. So I tied one on and started having success as well. Thanks Ken; those two flies will be in my box for a long time to come.

BECK'S HEX

Photo courtesy of Steve Erickson

MATERIALS

Designed by Steve Erickson (influenced by Gerry Beck)

Thread: UNI-Thread, 6/0, tan

Hook: Mustad 3906B, size 6

Tail: Grizzly Marabou, tan; and 2–3 strands of gold Krystal Flash

Body: Darkwater Dubbing, tan and brown mix

Hackle: Hungarian partridge

Rib: Gold wire, fine

Bead: Gold brass bead 3/16 in (3 mm)

1. De-barb the hook and slide on the gold bead.
2. Place the hook in the vice, start the thread behind the bead, and wrap back to the point of the barb.
3. Tie in the marabou tail. Length should equal the shank length.
4. Tie in the Krystal Flash along one side of the tail, then fold over and tie over the other side. Cut the flash to equal the tail length.
5. Tie in the fine gold wire.
6. Apply the dubbing to the thread, making a dubbing noodle that is approximately 8 in (20 cm) long. Place the dubbing twister halfway down the noodle and fold it back towards the hook. Twist the noodle tight and wrap towards the bead.
7. Tie off the dubbing noodle.
8. Wrap the ribbing 5 to 6 times along the shank of the hook and once the bead is reached tie it off.
9. Tie in a partridge feather by the tip, make two wraps, and tie off.
10. Whip finish behind the bead and coat the thread with UV epoxy to finish the fly.

STEVE'S TIP "This pattern originated with well-known Manitoba fly tyer and fisher Gerry Beck. It was made to imitate the plentiful *Hexagenia* nymphs found in much of Manitoba, which many fish will aggressively feed on. The heavy bead gets it to the bottom and then a rising motion imitates a nymph heading for the surface.

"This is my version of this fly, utilizing DDH dubbing and grizzly marabou to add colour and contrast to the pattern. It is particularly effective in the Red River below the dam at Lockport. Cast the fly upstream and allow it to sink to the bottom. Retrieve in short strips that will cause the fly to rise upward, imitating the nymph."

My first Pumpkinseed on a white DDH Leech with a gold bead.

WET FLIES

54	MARK'S PINK BEAD FLY
55	SALLY SOFT HACKLE
56	GH WET FLY
57	GROUSE AND ORANGE
58	GROUSE AND GREEN
60	MRS. SIMPSON
61	DRUNKEN NYMPH

Easy

Moderate

Difficult

WET FLIES

These flies are more of a traditional style of tying. Designed as a general representation of a nymph, these flies still catch fish regularly.

Scott Gardner of Outdoor Canada magazine with a terrific walleye on the fly.
Photo courtesy of Scott Gardner

MARK'S PINK BEAD FLY

MATERIALS

Designed by Mark Sandulak

Thread: Monocord, 3/0, fluorescent, pink

Hook: Tiemco 200R, size 14-10

Body: Glass beads, pink with silver insert

Hackle: Hungarian partridge

1. Pinch the barb down to enable the beads to slide onto the hook. The number of beads depends on the size of the hook.
2. Once the beads are on the hook, build up a butt section of pink monocord so the beads will not slide off.
3. Whip finish at the back of the hook, but do not cut the thread; advance the thread around the last bead and wrap 5 to 6 times between the last bead and the one in front. Repeat this process until you come to the front of the last bead at the eye of the hook.
4. Build up a thread base at the head of fly so the bead does not slip.
5. Tie in the partridge feather, do 2 wraps, then tie off.
6. When head cementing, run a drop of cement all along the body to cover the unprotected thread that is wrapped around and between the beads.

STU'S STORY This is a sleeper fly for huge rainbows in rivers and still water situations. Pink is one of those colours not widely used by fly fishermen for trout, but this fly has proven its worth. The best rainbow so far has been a 25-incher (63 cm).

I would like to thank Mark Sandulak for not only letting me use this fly but for tying it as well.

SALLY SOFT HACKLE

MATERIALS

Designed by Stu Thompson

Thread: Semperfli Nano Silk, 6/0, white (use an olive permanent marker to colour the thread)

Hook: Daiichi 1710, size 6-12

Tail: Mallard breast feather

Body: Darkwater Dubbing, olive

Hackle: Pheasant rump

1. Start the thread behind the hook eye and wrap back to the point of the barb.
2. Tie in a tail of mallard flank equal to the length of the shank of the hook.
3. Apply the dubbing to the thread and wrap forward to the eye of the hook building a nicely tapered body. Stop the thread approximately 1/16 in (1.5 mm) from the eye.
4. Choose a ringneck pheasant rump feather that is long enough to extend just past the hook bend and tie it in. Wrap the feather and tie it off.
5. When forming the head of the fly, feather the fibres back so they angle towards the bend of the hook. Whip finish and the fly is complete.

STU'S STORY This fly has taken numerous species of fish including carp, walleye, sauger, goldeye, mooneye, perch, all types of trout, and smallmouth bass. When fished during a mayfly hatch it is unbelievable. In still water situations, it can pass for a stickleback minnow.

GH WET FLY

MATERIALS

Designed by Gary Hanke; tied by Stu Thompson

Thread: Semperfli Nano Silk, 6/0, black

Hook: Mustad 3399, size 10 or equivalent

Tail: Black calf tail

Body: Peacock herl

Hackle: Guinea fowl

1. Start the thread at the eye of the hook and wrap back to the point of the barb.
2. Then tie in some black calf tail. The calf tail has to be long enough to extend past the bend of the hook one hook shank length, but also cover the shank of the hook to keep the same body diameter throughout the fly.
3. After securing the calf tail, wrap the thread back to the point of the barb and tie in 4 strands of peacock herl. Twist the herl together and wrap the body, stopping approximately 1/16 in (1.5 mm) before the eye, and tie the herl off.
4. Tie in a guinea fowl breast feather, the length of the fibres to equal one and a half times the hook gap, and wrap it forward towards the eye of the hook.
5. After tying off the feather, comb back the hackle fibres and form the head. Whip finish and the fly is done.

STU'S STORY This pattern was designed by Gary Hanke, an Alberta fly fisher. He is also the sales representative for Semperfli in Canada. He is, without a doubt, one of the best tyers this country has, winning numerous awards for his efforts.

A multitude of fish have been caught on this fly—everything from crappie and bluegill to carp and trout. I have even managed a few channel cats with this pattern as well.

GROUSE AND ORANGE

MATERIALS

Designed by Stu Thompson (Influenced by Sylvester Nemes)

Thread: Semperfli Nano Silk, 6/0, black

Hook: Daiichi 1550, size 10-14

Body: Darkwater Dubbing, sunrise orange

Hackle: Grouse breast feather

1. Place the hook in the vice and start the thread at the hook eye. Wrap the thread back to the point of the barb.
2. Apply the dubbing to the thread by placing a small amount on the thread and twist it with your thumb and index finger. Form a dubbing noodle that is approximately 3 in (7.5 cm).
3. Start wrapping the noodle back to the eye of the hook and building a tapered body.
4. When the body is complete, tie in a grouse breast feather and wrap the thread to the eye of the hook. Wrap the feather two to three times and tie off.
5. Comb all the fibres back so they flow past the bend of the hook. Wrap the thread over the fibres to hold them down and form the head of the fly. Whip finish and the fly is complete.

STU'S STORY There are times when this fly can be used as a searching pattern and at other times it makes an excellent caddis emerger. When the caddis hatch occurs, fish a dry line and cast to any visible fish. The resulting strikes will astound you. I also use this pattern quite regularly in late autumn. The reason for this is orange is a trigger colour for some species of fish, most notably walleye and brown trout.

GROUSE AND GREEN

MATERIALS — *Designed by Stu Thompson (Influenced by Sylvester Nemes)*

Thread: Semperfli Nano Silk, 6/0, black

Hook: Daiichi 1550, size 8-14

Body: Ice Dub peacock, black

Hackle: Grouse breast feather

1. Pace the hook in the vice and start the thread at the eye of the hook. Wrap the thread to the point of the barb and let approximately 4 in of thread out from the bobbin.
2. Apply the dubbing, spinning it onto the thread.
3. Wrap the dubbing noodle towards the eye of the hook, stopping approximately 1/16 inch (1.5 mm) from the eye.
4. Tie in the grouse feather. The fibres of the feather have to extend just past the bend of the hook.
5. Wrap the feather 2 to 3 times and tie off.
6. Comb all the fibres back and secure them with thread wraps.
7. Form the head and whip finish.

STU'S STORY I'll never forget the first time I met Sylvester Nemes. I was 24 and attending my first Federation of Fly Fishers Conclave, and was in heaven. I noticed him tying some soft hackles and that really intrigued me. Little did I realize who I was talking to, a distinguished author nonetheless. Talk about a bonus: I spent the entire three hours at his table asking questions and getting answers for every question I asked. Unbelievable! Needless to say I bought two of his books and I still use his techniques today some 40 years later. I have caught virtually every species of fish in the province with typical wet flies. Doesn't matter when you fish them or even where but Sylvester was right as he told me, "They will work anytime, anywhere." No truer statement has been made. Even managed a few channel cats with this pattern as well.

The author with a bulldog of a channel cat caught on the Red River.

MRS. SIMPSON

MATERIALS — *Designer unknown, tied by Stu Thompson*

Thread: Semperfli Nano Silk, 6/0, black
Hook: Daiichi 1710 or equivalent, size 4-12
Tail: Calf tail, black
Body: Wool, red
Wing: Hungarian partridge, olive

1. Start the thread at the eye of the hook and wrap back to the point of the barb.
2. Tie in the black calf tail, ensuring the butt ends are long enough to reach the eye of the hook.
3. Advance the thread in close wraps to the eye of the hook and trim the calf tail.
4. Wrap the thread back to the point of the barb and tie in the first pair of partridge wings (one on each side of the hook).
5. Tie in a piece of red wool and advance the thread halfway up the hook shank. Wrap the wool to this point and tie off.
6. Then add the second pair of partridge wings (again one on each side). Tie in the wool again and advance it to the eye of the hook, remembering to leave enough room to form the head of the fly.
7. Tie off the wool and lay the last wings of partridge in place (one on each side). Form the head and whip finish.

STU'S STORY This fly was originated in New Zealand, but it has proven itself time and again in my home waters. Lake trout, rainbows, browns, brookies, smallmouth, sauger, and walleye have all fallen victim to this pattern. The most success is when fishing around shorelines that contain fist-sized boulders or some downed logs. Casting to and retrieving through these structures is very rewarding.

DRUNKEN NYMPH

MATERIALS

Designed by Stephen Jay

Thread: UNI-Thread, 8/0, wine

Hook: Daiichi 1550, size 8-12

Tail: Guinea fowl fibres, claret

Body: Darkwater Dubbing, champagne

Rib: Red flat tinsel, small

Hackle: Hungarian partridge, claret

1. Place the hook in the vice and start the thread at the eye of the hook and wrap back to the point of the barb.
2. Tie in about a dozen claret guinea fowl fibres to extend a hook shank length past the bend of the hook, then tie in the tinsel for the rib.
3. Let out approximately 5 in (12 cm) of thread and apply the dubbing in a one-directional spinning motion with the thumb and index finger.
4. Wrap the newly formed dubbing noodle towards the eye of the hook, stopping about 1/8 inch (3 mm) from the eye, and tie off.
5. Wrap the ribbing forward with about 4 or 5 wraps and tie off where the dubbing was tied off.
6. Tie in the claret partridge feather and wrap 2 to 3 times.
7. Tie off the feather and comb the fibres back.
8. Wrap the thread around the combed back fibres and secure.
9. Form the head and whip finish.

STEPHEN'S TIP "I have fished this pattern in British Columbia and Manitoba, targeting small creek waters holding browns, rainbows, cutthroats, and tigers, and have had great success with it. There is something effective about purple like colours for salmonids. Cast upstream and drift through a hole or cast down and pull through a likely holding area and it will entice strikes. Great pattern for those considering Tenkara."

DRY FLIES

64   **MIKE'S MAYFLY**

66   **MIKE'S PARACHUTE MAYFLY**

68   **MIKE'S HEXAGENIA**

Easy

Moderate

Difficult

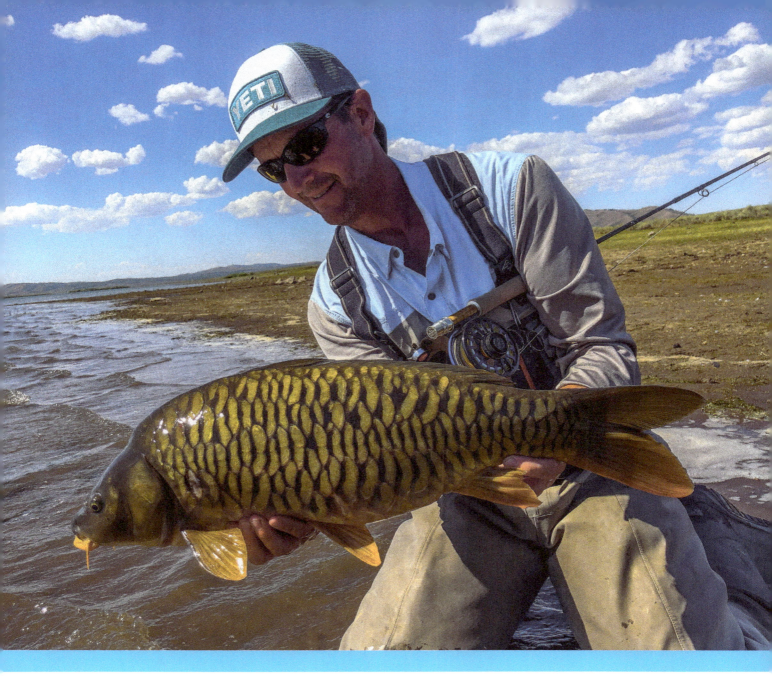

DRY FLIES

The adult stage of the aquatic insects relates to five percent of the fish's diet. When there is a hatch, there are thousands of adult insects on the water and if you present the fly properly in the feeding lane of the fish, it will take it and the fight is on.

Jeff Currier with a beautiful carp.
Photo courtesy of Jeff Currier

MIKE'S MAYFLY

MATERIALS

Designed by Mike Corrigan

Thread: UNI-Thread, 6/0, olive

Hook: Daiichi 112, size 14-16

Tail: Microfibetts

Body: Hareline Velvet Chenille, dark olive

Wing: Silver Tip Fly Company "mayfly wing"

Dubbing: Darkwater Dubbing, dark olive

Hackle: Natural grizzly

1. Create the body by singeing a small portion of velvet chenille in a candle flame to taper one end.
2. Cut the burned portion of the chenille to expose the core.
3. Thread a small needle through the center of the chenille (tapered end).
4. Once the point of the needle is through the chenille, take 2 or 3 Microfibetts and thread the blunt ends through the eye of the needle.
5. Pull the needle through the rest of the chenille.
6. The pointed end of the Microfibetts will be sticking out the tapered end of the body. Adjust them to the desired length.
7. Place the hook in the vice and wrap the thread from the eye of the hook to the point of the barb.
8. Take the body that was made from the steps above and tie it in with several wraps of thread to secure it in place.
9. Wrap the thread halfway up the hook shank and tie in the Silver Tip mayfly wings with figure-eight wraps.
10. Tie in a grizzly hackle where the body was tied in and secure it with a few wraps of thread.
11. Apply the dubbing to the thread and build up a thorax
12. Wrap the hackle behind and in front of the wings.
13. Tie off the hackle.
14. Form a small thread head and whip finish.

MIKE'S TIP The profile of this fly makes for a perfect imitation when smaller mayflies are hatching. The endless sizes and colour combinations make for a great match to the hatch choice. This pattern may also be tied in a spent wing style, with a foam parachute post or hackle-less. A word of caution when using the larger sized Silver Tip wings: the fly will tend to spin, causing leader twist or kinking. (Use 3 x tippet or larger.)

When the mayfly hatches occur in Manitoba, just about every species of fish will feed on them. From perch and crappie to rainbows and browns, all can be caught at one time or another when the timing is right.

Colin McKeown, of The New Fly Fisher, with a massive smallmouth on the fly.

Photo courtesy of The New Fly Fisher

MIKE'S PARACHUTE MAYFLY

MATERIALS

Designed by Mike Corrigan

Thread: UNI-Thread, 6/0, olive

Hook: Daiichi 1120, size 14-18

Tail: Microfibetts

Body: Hareline Velvet Chenille, dark olive

Wing: Antron, fluorescent pink or white

Dubbing: Darkwater Dubbing, olive

Hackle: Grizzly, dyed olive

1. Create the body by singeing a small portion of velvet chenille in a candle flame to taper one end. Cut the burned portion of the chenille to expose the core.
2. Thread a small needle through the centre of the chenille (tapered end). Once the point of the needle is through the chenille, take 2 or 3 Microfibetts and thread the blunt ends through the eye of the needle.
3. Pull the needle through the rest of the chenille. The pointy ends of the Microfibetts should be sticking out the rear of the body; adjust them to the desired length.
4. Place the hook in the vice and wrap the thread from the eye of the hook to the point of the barb.
5. Attach the newly created body (above) with several wraps of thread.
6. Tie in the Antron for the parachute wing by lying it flat and securing it to the hook shank.
7. Roll the Antron between your thumb and index finger and wrap the thread horizontally up the post about 1/8 in (2 to 3 mm).
8. Tie in the hackle at the base of the post, leaving a bit of the stem.
9. Apply the dubbing to the thread in a one-directional spinning motion and build up a thorax.
10. Do 6 wraps of hackle, wrapping 3 times up the post and 3 times down.
11. Tie the hackle off at the eye of the hook.
12. Form a small head, whip finish, and the fly is complete.

MIKE'S TIP "What is amazing about this pattern is that it can be tied in any colour combination to imitate any and all of the smaller species of mayfly. This fly will catch all species of trout, lake whitefish, tullibee, goldeye, mooneye, and when the hatch is thick enough, this pattern has also taken walleye, and sauger".

A nice-looking splake, a cross between a lake trout and a brook trout, caught by the author while fishing on one of his favourite lakes.

MIKE'S HEXAGENIA

MATERIALS
Designed by Mike Corrigan

Thread: UNI-Thread, 6/0, brown; and clear mono (invisible thread)

Hook: Eagle Claw L042, wide gap, size 8

Tail: Foam, 1/8 in (3 mm), brown, over 1/16 in (2 mm), tan

Body: Darkwater Dubbing, bloody black

Wing: Antron, white; or MFC Widow's Web

Hackle: brown

1. Create the body on a tube fly-tying tool. Wrap the clear mono on the two pieces of foam (brown over tan) to build the 8 or 9 segments required. Wrap the thread at a 45-degree angle to the end of the body and repeat in the opposite direction. Half hitch and set aside. Microfibetts can be added if desired.

2. Place the hook in the vice and wrap the brown thread towards the rear of the hook, stopping at the point of the barb.

3. Tie in the foam body, dark brown on top, by wrapping the thread towards the eye.

4. Add the wing by tying the Antron on top of the shank, midway between the eye of the hook and the tail. The Antron has to be tied in the middle, then folded back and over-wrapped to be secured.

5. Tie in the hackle, but do not wrap it.

6. Apply the dubbing to the thread and wrap the dubbing behind and in front of the wing.

7. Wrap the hackle through the dubbing with wraps in front and behind the wing.

8. Form the head, whip finish, and the fly is complete.

MIKE'S TIP "The profile of this fly makes for a great imitation when the *Hexagenia* mayfly hatch is on. Bass, whitefish, goldeye, mooneye, sauger, walleye, and even channel cats will feed on this insect. The hatches in Manitoba average 4.2 tonnes per year and will peak the second or third week of June".

Not the largest but still a lot of fun on the fly rod. This largemouth bass was taken on a white DDH Leech.

POPPERS

72	MIKEY MOUSE
74	STEVE'S SLIDER
75	THE LEAF
76	SE FOAM POPPER
78	TIGER'S TAIL POPPER
80	JIG-A-POP
82	KERMIT
84	THE TERMINATOR
85	BASS DIVER

Easy

Moderate

Difficult

The smile says it all. Jenna McKeown, of The New Fly Fisher, with a fantastic smallmouth.
Photo courtesy of The New Fly Fisher

POPPERS

The topwater bait for fly fishers, these flies can be tied to represent mice, frogs, or anything else fish feed on. There is nothing as exciting as watching a vicious topwater strike!

MIKEY MOUSE

MATERIALS

Designed by Mike Corrigan

Thread: UNI-Thread, 6/0, tan
Hook: Daiichi 2220 4XL, size 6
Tail: Ultra Chenille, tan
Body: Bernat Boa yarn, tan
Over-body: Craft foam, tan
Ears: Craft foam, tan
Head: Darkwater Dubbing, tan
Eyes: 3D, 1/8 in (3 mm)

1. Before tying, prepare the foam by cutting the body in the shape of an oval, approximately 1 in by 1/2 in (25 mm by 12 mm). Cut the ears using a Chernobyl body foam cutter, or freelance it 1/4 in by 1/2 in (5 mm by 10 mm) with a curved end. Also at this time, prepare the tail by selecting a piece of Ultra Chenille and singeing one end.
2. Place the hook in the vice, start the thread at the eye of the hook, and wrap back to the point of the barb.
3. Tie in the tail of Ultra Chenille with the singed end extending beyond the hook bend.
4. Tie in the foam over-body at the point of the barb by pinching the foam together at one end and wrapping over the foam to secure it.
5. Tie in the Bernat Boa at the same juncture and advance the thread to the halfway point of the shank.
6. Wrap the body material to the thread and tie off.
7. Pull the foam body forward and tie down at the midpoint of the shank.
8. Add the ears (one on each side) by pinching one end and securing with thread wraps.
9. Let out approximately 3 in (7.5 cm) of thread and apply the Darkwater Dubbing by spinning it on the thread.
10. Build up the head with the newly formed dubbing noodle.
11. After the head is complete, whip finish.
12. Add a drop of Krazy Glue Gel on the head where you want to place the eyes.
13. Press the eyes on and allow to dry.

MIKE'S TIP "This fly was originated for the New Zealand mouse infestation, which happens every three to five years. With its proven success in New Zealand, I decided to try it for tiger trout at Twin Lake and what a discovery. The tigers have jumped all over this topwater fly and it has become my go-to pattern. When fishing this fly, cast and move the tip of the rod in a side to side motion with a slow retrieve. You may also tie this pattern in other colours."

"The proof is in the pudding" as the old saying goes. A nice tiger that Mike Corrigan caught by using a Mikey Mouse.

STEVE'S SLIDER

Photo courtesy of Steve Erickson

MATERIALS

Designed by Steve Erickson

Thread: UNI-Thread, 6/0, tan

Hook: Tiemco 8089, size 10

Tail: Marabou, yellow and Krystal Flash, pearl

Body: Crystal chenille, chartreuse, and 5 segments of 1/16 in (2 mm) craft foam (trapezoids approximately 1/2 in x 1/4 in (10 mm x 7 mm), yellow

Legs: Round rubber hackle, yellow

1. Place the hook in the vice, start the thread at the eye of the hook, and continue to the point of the barb.
2. Tie in the marabou tail; length should equal the shank of the hook.
3. Tie in 6 strands of pearl Krystal Flash along one side of the tail. Fold over the Krystal Flash and tie down on the other side of the tail. Cut the flash to equal the marabou tail.
4. Tie in the crystal chenille at the back of the hook.
5. Select and prepare 5 pieces of craft foam to tie in. To make these sections, start by cutting a 1/2-in-wide (10-mm-wide) strip from the foam sheet. Then cut the strip crosswise at alternating angles to create matching trapezoids.
6. Tie in each piece of foam by folding it over the hook, with the narrower part of the trapezoid toward the eye, and thread just in front of the foam. Tie the thread back over the foam to solidly secure it into place.
7. Tie in 3 sections of foam and then tie in the rubber legs with figure-eight wraps.
8. Tie in the remaining two pieces of foam in front of the rubber legs.
9. Carefully wind the crystal chenille over the body, wrapping between the foam segments.
10. Tie off the crystal chenille and form the head. After whip finishing, coat the thread with UV epoxy.

STEVE'S TIP "I tie this with a simple marabou tail, and usually in yellow as I have had great success with this subtler version of this pattern. But it can be modified to any set of colours, etc. to add flash or attraction. I have had a lot of success with smallmouth that didn't seem interested in more aggressive poppers.

Cast to a structure and allow to rest; often bass will strike after this pause. Give 2 or 3 sharp strips and pause again; bass often delay the strike, so a few seconds pause has increased my success rate significantly."

THE LEAF

MATERIALS

Designed by Mike Corrigan

Thread: Clear mono (invisible thread)

Hook: Gamakatsu SC-15 2H, size 2/0 or 3/0

Tail: Carded 100% acrylic yarn, orange (see page 190)

Body: SAAP body fur or Bernat Boa, orange

Over-body: 1/4 in. (5-6mm) thick craft foam cut 2 in x 3.5 in (1.5 x 9 cm)

Eyes: 1/8 in (3-4mm) eyes made using melted mono and UV epoxy

1. Place the hook in the vice and start the thread at the eye, wrapping back to the point of the barb.
2. Tie in the tail of acrylic carded yard approximately 4 or 5 inches (10–12 cm), then add a drop of Krazy Glue.
3. Cut a point in the end of the foam and tie it in with the wide portion of the foam pointing past the bend of the hook.
4. Tie in the body material and wrap it to the thread point, which is approximately 1/8 in (3 mm) from the eye.
5. Tie off the body material and secure with thread wraps.
6. Apply the eyes with figure-eight wraps until secure.
7. Pull the foam over body forward, but leave extra near the bend of the hook by first pushing it backward to create the large butt. Tie off and add a drop of Krazy Glue. Leave an overhang of foam approximately 1/2 in (8–10 mm) beyond the eye of the hook to allow for a "pop" when moved in the water.

MIKE'S TIP "The fly is meant to imitate something (not sure what) on the surface of the water for late-season musky. We observed fish "striking leaves" in the fall in an attempt to find food. Cast and move the fly a few times and leave it."

I think I have an idea about how Mike fishes this fly, but let me tell you it sure does catch largemouth, smallmouth, and pike like crazy. I also tie this in red and white, and chartreuse and black. No matter what colour, it works.

NOTE The eyes are optional.

SE FOAM POPPER

MATERIALS

Designed by Steve Erickson

Thread: Semperfli Nano Silk, black, 6/0

Hook: Mustad CK 52S, size 2-4

Tail: Saddle hackle, 4 pieces and Flashabou

Body: High-density foam cut from a pair of flip-flops

Body colours: Permanent markers

Legs: Rubber hackle, round

1. Carve a body from foam and attach it to the hook with Krazy Glue (see tying tips below).
2. Tie in 10 strands of Flashabou for the centre of the tail.
3. Tie in two feathers on each side, curved out and away from the hook. Do not cut off the butt section of the excess hackle. Instead, wrap the thread to the back of the body and wind the base of the feathers to make a thick hackle behind the body.
4. Tie off the hackles and then secure the thread behind the body with a whip finish.
5. Attach the legs through the body by using a heavy needle to pull them through the foam body from side to side.

STEVE'S TYING TIP "The first I learned of this pattern was from the Manitoba Fly Fishers Association club meeting about fishing for smallmouth bass. A pattern was presented by Steve Abrahams in the club newsletter, and variations on it are common. Popular colours include yellow, green, white, pink, but just about any colour will work.

"The foam used is a high-density EVA foam from a beach flip-flop sandal. This tough foam is resilient but shapeable, and it stays on the hook very well. While this foam is found in some applications other than sandals, it is worth paying attention to the type of foam, as many other kinds of foam do not have the same properties. It is available in many colours and holds marker colour well. A single pair of sandals can make dozens of bodies for the popper.

"To make the body, the foam is initially shaped by carving roughly with a snap blade knife. The body is then smoothed and the shaping finished using a rotary tool with an abrasive head. Alternatively, the foam can be fixed onto a spindle and placed in a drill or rotary tool to form a high-speed lathe. In this case, a nail file or sandpaper can be used to shape the body as it spins. In either case, the resulting body can be attached to the hook by adding glue to the hook shank and feeding the body over, curving it around the hook, or by making a

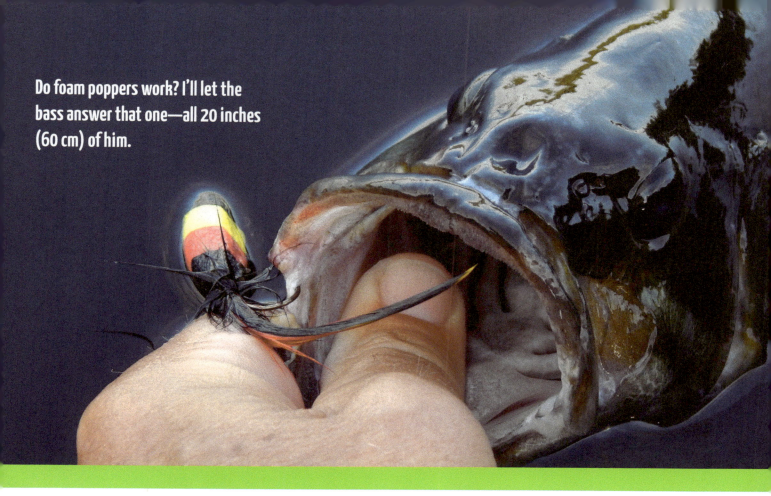

Do foam poppers work? I'll let the bass answer that one—all 20 inches (60 cm) of him.

slit in the body with a razor blade and gluing the hook into the slit.

The depth of cavity at the front of the body will determine how much 'pop' the fly has in the water. I will use bodies having a variety of depths, including simple flat-fronted versions."

STEVE'S TIP "A great fly for fishing smallmouth bass in the early summer. Cast into shore or cover and allow to sit. Give it a couple of sharp strips to make it pop. Try different retrieves to get different surface effects. Nothing beats seeing bass smash these poppers on the surface."

TIGER'S TAIL POPPER

MATERIALS

Designed by Stu Thompson

Thread: Semperfli Nano Silk, 6/0, white

Hook: Daiichi 1550, size 2

Tail: Zonker strip, tiger

Head: Deer body hair; yellow, orange and black

Eyes: 1/4 in (6 mm) silver with black pupil

1. Place the hook in the vice, start the tread at the eye of the hook, and wrap back to the point of the barb.
2. Tie in the zonker strip and build a thread ramp so the body hair can spin.
3. Take a generous clump of yellow deer body hair and comb out the underfur.
4. Place the hair on top of the hook shank and do 2 loose wraps around it. Push the hair around the hook shank then pull the thread down tight.
5. Place a clump of orange hair on top of the yellow and hold in place with 2 loose wraps of thread.
6. Place a small clump of black body hair on top of the orange and hold in place with 2 loose wraps of thread.
7. Pull down tight on the thread hold the deer body hair in place.
8. After the hair flairs, comb it back, and do 5 wraps of thread in front of the hair.
9. Repeat this process until the eye of the hook is reached.
10. Trim the hair to the desired shape and cut the eye sockets.
11. Place a dollop of Goop in the sockets and press the eyes on.
12. Place the fly in a piece of foam and allow to dry.

STU'S TIP This fly is extremely effective for pike, bass, and musky and can be fished at any depth or on the surface. It is quite thrilling to see these fish come up and take this fly. You never know when it will happen and when it does the adrenalin rush is awesome.

A 22-in (55 cm) brown trout caught by my son, Kevin, on a Mallard SB.

JIG-A-POP

MATERIALS

Designed by Stu Thompson

Thread: Semperfli Nano Silk, 6/0, white

Hook: Mustad 32833NP-BN, size 10-4/0

Tail: Hackle; black, red, and yellow

Body: Deer body hair; yellow, black, and red

1. Place the hook in the vice, start the thread at the eye of the hook, and wrap back to the point of the barb.
2. Tie in 2 black hackle feathers, one on each side.
3. Tie in 2 red hackle feathers in front of the black, one on each side.
4. Finally, tie in 2 yellow hackle feathers in front of the red, one on each side.
5. Take a generous clump of yellow deer body hair and comb out the underfur.
6. Place the body hair on top of the hook shank and hold in place with two loose wraps of thread.
7. Push down on the hair to encompass the whole hook shank. Pull the thread down tight and do 5 more wraps of thread through the body hair.
8. Comb all the fibres back and do 5 wraps of thread in front of the hair.
9. Get another clump of yellow and apply it by holding the hair on a 45-degree angle to the hook shank. Do 2 loose wraps then pull down tight releasing the hair so it can spin.
10. Do 4 clumps of yellow hair then compress the hair by pushing the hair back towards the bend. Hold your thumb and forefinger of your left hand at the back of the first clump of hair; then with your right thumb and forefinger, push back on the hair to compress.
11. Apply a generous clump of black body hair to the hook by spinning it just as with the yellow.
12. Apply a clump of red to the hook shank and spin it on. At this time, the tyer should have reached the 90-degree bend in the jig hook.
13. Take the hook out of the vice and turn it so the exposed bend is sitting horizontal.
14. Add another clump of red at this point. It will spin, no problem.
15. Apply the last clump of red body hair, comb the fibres back, and do 5 wraps in front of the hair.
16. Whip finish at the eye of the hook.
17. Cut and trim to desired shape.

Can you imagine a 40-in (1 m) pike slamming a Jig-A-Pop? I can and it is completely AWESOME! There is no describing the feeling you get when you see a monster like this coming to your fly.

STU'S TIP Why did I tie a deer hair popper on a jig hook? How many times have you gone out bass fishing and cast a popper only to have the popper skip over the surface instead of making a popping sound? If you are like me, it is an awful lot. I found it frustrating not being able to get the popper to do what I wanted it to, so as a result I came up with this solution and it has worked like a dream. If you look at this popper, where is the hook eye pointing? Straight down. Where is your leader when this popper is sitting on the water? It's underneath the surface as soon as the fly lands on the water. Can you pop it once you cast? You better believe it! No more waiting for your leader to sink; you can start working the fly as fast as you want or as slow as you want instantaneously. It's awesome!

KERMIT

MATERIALS — Designed by Mike Corrigan

Thread: Clear mono (invisible thread)

Hook: Gamakatsu SC-15 2H, size 2/0 or equivalent

Head: 1/4 in (5 mm) craft foam, cut 1/2 x 1 in (2 cm x 3 cm), chartreuse

Legs: 100% acrylic yarn, carded (see page 188), chartreuse; and 1/8 in (4 mm) diameter shrink tubing (size is prior to shrinking) by 1 in (2.5 cm) long, clear

Body: Crosscut rabbit strips, chartreuse

Rubber Legs: LazerScales, 3 per side (folded in half), chartreuse

Eyes: 1/4 in (6 mm) 3D silver with black pupil

1. Create the legs by cutting 10 strands of 100% acrylic yarn, approximately 10 in (25 cm) in length; tie a knot in the middle.

2. Using a self-healing cutting board, comb the yarn with a dog brush. Start with the tips of the yarn on one side of the knot and work your way towards the knot until all the yarn is fluffy.

3. Repeat this for the other side of the yarn. As a result, you will have enough leg material for quite a few flies.

4. Using a bobbin threader (or a loop of monofilament), feed a section of the carded yarn into the shrink tubing.

5. Once the yarn is in place, heat the shrink tubing with a candle to secure the yarn; adding a drop of Krazy Glue in the tube will ensure the yarn won't pull out.

6. Fold the foam in half (long dimension) and mark the centre. Use the hook point to poke the middle of the fold of foam and slide the foam to the eye. Centre the foam and while holding it in place add some Krazy Glue, squeeze the foam until it is secured to the hook shank, and let dry.

7. Put the hook in the vice and add the legs; they should be positioned on either side of the shank. Secure with the thread.

8. At the back of the hook, just where the shank bends down, pull the legs to the side so that the shrink tubing bends. Keep tightening the thread and secure the legs. Add a drop of Krazy Glue to the thread wraps.

9. Tie in the crosscut rabbit strip, with the hair pointing backwards, and wrap towards the head. Do not leave any gaps. Tie the off rabbit strip and trim.

10. Add 3, 2-to-3-in (6-to-8-cm) pieces of LazerScales rubber legs to each side. Tie in at midpoint of each clump so that there are 6 legs on each side. The legs should be 1 to 1 1/2 in (3 to 4 cm) when done.

11. Whip finish and add another drop of Krazy Glue.

12. Apply the eyes with Krazy Glue Gel and trim the corners of the head. The fly is finished.

Photo courtesy of Keith Sinfield

MIKE'S TIP "This fly rides butt down, just as the natural frog does. When retrieved, it darts to the side and the legs add realism to this frog pattern. As well, the large head on this popper will move a lot of water, creating more disturbance and attracting more fish because of the vibrations created. Used close to shore along weed beds, it is a great pattern for pike, musky, and smallmouth bass. Don't be afraid to try it for other species of fish as well".

KEITH SINFIELD is a relative newcomer to the sport, but let me tell you—his thought process is out of this world. He has taken to tying like a duck to water and he has come up with some truly amazing flies. The great thing about his patterns is that the size can be adapted to fit any species of fish, and they work. His Musky Killer and Zonker flies have taken some truly tremendous brown and rainbow trout, especially in the months of September and October. Not only that, but a host of warm-water species have all fallen for his creations. He has also taken some well-known patterns and changed the colour combinations and has caught fish like crazy. Keith is the type of guy you want to get to know because his understanding of colours is out of this world and he has proven it over and over.

THE TERMINATOR

MATERIALS

Designed by Mike Corrigan

Thread: Clear mono (invisible thread)

Hook: Daiichi 2546, size 2-1/0

Over-body: 1/4 in (5–6 mm) craft foam, chartreuse. Taper foam from 1/2 in. (14 mm) to 1/4 in. (5 mm). The length should be several cm longer than the shank of the hook.

Tail: Rabbit zonker strip, chartreuse with black tips

Body: Crosscut rabbit strip, chartreuse

Eyes: Medium dumbbell

Throat: Bernat Boa or SAAP body fur, red

1. Place the hook in the vice and start the thread at the eye of the hook. Wrap back to the point of the barb and then back to the eye of the hook.
2. Add the dumbbell eyes on top of the hook shank using figure-eight wraps; leave a 1/16 in (2 mm) gap near the eye of the hook to tie in the foam. Add a drop of Krazy Glue to secure.
3. Take the thread to the point of the barb and tie in the zonker strip tail. Length to be one and a half to two times the shank of the hook. Add another drop of Krazy Glue to secure.
4. Tie in the crosscut rabbit strip at the bend of the hook, with the hair of the strip pointing to the bend.
5. Tie in the wider part of the tapered foam on top of the crosscut rabbit, leaving a minimum 1/2 inch (1 cm) of foam overhang.
6. Pull the foam back and wrap the crosscut rabbit strip to the dumbbell eyes.
7. Pull the foam down, secure it in front of the eyes, and trim.
8. Add the red throat in front of the eyes on the underside of the shank; add a drop of Krazy Glue to secure.

MIKE'S TIP "This fly was originally designed for tarpon as it is a neutral buoyancy pattern. Tarpon have their mouths facing upward and only take food within the upper portion of the water column. Bass, pike, and trout take this as a minnow pattern. Other colours will work as well. Use a dry line when fishing this fly".

NOTE If 1/4 in (5 mm) foam is unavailable, widen the head so that the buoyancy of the foam is the same (the extra width will make up for reduced thickness). Thinner foam can be glued together to build up the thickness.

BASS DIVER

MATERIALS

Designed by Stu Thompson (influenced by Larry Dahlberg)

Thread: Semperfli Nano Silk, 3/0, white

Hook: Daiichi 2546. size 2-4/0

Tail: Neck hackle, purple

Head: Spun deer body hair, trimmed to shape

Eyes: Gold with a black pupil

1. Place the hook in the vice, start the thread at the eye of the hook, and wrap back to the point of the barb.
2. Select 4 hackles and tie them in at the back of the hook. Place 2 hackles on one side and secure with 5 to 6 wraps of thread. Repeat the process for the other side.
3. Take a very generous amount of deer body hair and comb out the underfur.
4. Place the clump of hair on the hook and push it down to surround the hook.
5. Do 2 loose wraps and pull down tight. The hair will flair all around the hook shank. Wrap the thread through this clump of body hair 5 or 6 more times.
6. Comb all the hair back and wrap the thread in front of the hair.
7. Take another clump, combing out the underfur beforehand, and place it on a 45-degree angle to the hook. Do 2 loose wraps and as the hair starts to flare out, let it go and it will spin, encompassing the whole hook shank.
8. Compact the first and second clump by pushing on the hair so it is squeezed against the first clump.
9. Continue adding and compressing the deer body hair until the hook shank is covered.
10. Whip finish the thread.
11. Take the fly out of the vice and trim the bottom flat with a single-edge razor blade. Trim the rest of the head with a pair of curved hair scissors. Leave a collar at the back of the head.
12. Cut the eye sockets and apply a dollop of goop in each socket. Place the eyes in the sockets and press firmly.

STU'S TIP Bass, pike, musky, and even the occasional walleye have all fallen victim to this fly. Easy to tie. Easy to fish. I absolutely love fishing this fly around beaver lodges: bass just show up out of nowhere and hit it. Not only that, but I have used this fly on brown trout lakes in the same location and have done extremely well with it.

STREAMERS

88	THE BLOB
90	BECKY'S BLACK STRIP LEECH
91	PINK ZONKER
93	EASTER EGG BUGGER
94	THE SAWICH KILLER
96	CLARET TIGER LEECH
97	MYMINNOW
98	DeROSE DACE
100	MALLARD SB
103	BENDBACK MINNOW BLACK AND ORANGE
104	WHATIZIT
105	ERICKSON'S CLOUSER
106	KEVIN'S LEECH
107	TOKARYK KILLER
109	DDH LEECH
110	RED RIVER SHINER
111	SRT STICKLEBACK
112	BOU BUG
114	ERIKSON'S DREAM
116	STU'S SCULPIN
118	ZEKE'S NIGHTMARE
121	BRIGETTE'S BADASS BAITFISH
122	MANITOBA MATUKA
123	ROLLED MUDDLER
124	LOCKPORT STANDARD
125	DDH EYES NATURAL GREY
128	DDH EYES WHITE MINNOW
130	DDH HEAD PURPLE AND PINK

Easy
Moderate
Difficult

STREAMERS

Some streamers are tied to imitate baitfish or leeches, while others are tied not to represent anything except bright colours. No matter which one you use, chances are you will catch fish on them—my favourite type of fly to fish.

Mike Corrigan holding a 38-in (1-m) channel cat.

THE BLOB

MATERIALS

Designed by Stu Thompson

Thread: Semperfli Nano Silk, 3/0, white (coloured with an olive marker)

Hook: Daiichi 1710, size 8-12

Tail: Darkwater Dubbing, olive

Body: Darkwater Dubbing, olive

Head: Gold bead (size determines how fast you want the fly to sink) or orange glass bead

1. De-barb the hook and slide the bead to the eye of the hook.
2. Place the hook in the vice, start the thread right behind the bead, and wrap it to the point of the barb.
3. Tie in a tail of Darkwater Dubbing.
4. Let out approximately 6 in (15 cm) of thread, place the dubbing twister halfway, then fold the thread back towards the hook shank.
5. Wrap 5 to 6 turns of thread to lock the dubbing loop into place, then advance the thread to the bead.
6. Take the dubbing mixture, place it crosswise in the loop, and twist tight.
7. Brush out any loose fibres with a small battery brush.
8. Wrap the dubbing noodle to the back of the bead.
9. Tie the noodle off, form the head, and the fly is complete.

STU'S TIP People look at this fly and they shake their heads. I guess they think that this fly doesn't catch fish. I can tell you after fishing this fly for 40 years, it certainly does catch fish. It is absolutely amazing how many different species I have caught using this fly. Here is the list: channel cat, bullheads, carp, big mouth buffalo, goldeye, mooneye, sauger, walleye, smallmouth bass, white bass, rainbows, browns, brookies, lake whitefish, freshwater drum, silver redhorse (suckers), grayling, perch, crappie, bluegill, splake, tiger trout, and rock bass. All on a blob of dubbing. In a river situation, this fly can be dead drifted or fished like a typical streamer with an up and across presentation. While in lakes, I have crawled this pattern across the bottom and fished it high in the water column. Any method will work with this fly.

The results from an orange Blob.

THE BLOB As you can see, this pattern can be tied in any colour with any type of dubbing you want; the number of different colours is infinite. The colours above are the most productive for me. I do switch between gold beads and orange glass beads.

BECKY'S BLACK STRIP LEECH

MATERIALS — *Designed by Stu Thompson (influenced by Dan Byford)*

Tread: Semperfli Nano Silk, 3/0, black

Hook: Daiichi 1720, size 2-12

Body: Rayon chenille, black ; and chenille, red

Wing: Rabbit zonker strip, black

1. Place the hook in the vice and start the thread at the eye of the hook. Wrap back to the point of the barb.
2. Select the rabbit strip for the wing and measure for the length of the tail, which is 1/8 to 1/4 in (3 to 6mm) past the bend.
3. Separate the hair and secure with the thread, wrapping around the shank and hide of the strip.
4. Fold the zonker strip over the bend of the hook and tie in the black rayon chenille.
5. Wrap the chenille forward, stopping approximately 1/4 inch (6 mm) from the hook eye, then tie off.
6. Tie in the red chenille, do 2 complete wraps, and then tie it off.
7. Bring the zonker strip forward and tie down.
8. Form the head and whip finish.

STU'S TIP This is one of the first leech patterns I ever used and it still proves effective to this day. Although it can be tied in a multitude of colours, my best two are the one pictured above and an olive colour. Out of the 32 game fish species listed for my home province, this pattern has caught 27 of them. I will fish this pattern in a tandem rig setup and numerous times have had two fish on at a time.

BONUS FLY

PINK ZONKER

MATERIALS — Designed by Stu Thompson (influenced by Dan Byford)

Thread: Monocord 3/0, fluorescent pink

Hook: Daiichi 1710, size 2-10

Body: Darkwater Dubbing, fluorescent pink

Wing: Zonker strip, fluorescent pink

Tag: Copper wire

1. Place the hook in the vice, start the thread at the eye of the hook, and wrap to the point of the barb.
2. Tie in a piece of copper wire and secure the tag end with wraps of thread.
3. Place the zonker strip on top of the hook shank and measure the tail, which is one hook shank length.
4. Separate the hair and secure the zonker strip with 3 very tight wraps of copper wire. Advance the wire to the thread and tie it off.
5. Flip the zonker strip over the back of the hook and prepare for the body.
6. Wrap the thread back to the point of the barb and form a dubbing loop by letting out approximately 8 in (20 cm) of thread out and then placing the dubbing twister at the halfway point of the thread. Fold the thread up towards the hook and wrap the thread back to the eye.
7. Place the dubbing mixture crosswise in the loop and twist tight.
8. Remove any loose fibres with a small battery brush or a Velcro brush.
9. Wrap the dubbing noodle forward and tie off. Cut the top of the dubbed body off then bring the zonker strip over. Tie the zonker strip down, trim off, and form the head with the thread. Whip finish and the fly is complete.

STU'S TIP A person may think we have salmon or steelhead in our province, but alas we do not. What we do have are warm-water species that love the colour pink. Some of my best channel cats have come on pink, not to mention pike, walleye, bass (white, smallmouth, and largemouth), carp, and even the odd whitefish. When it comes to trout, I will fish this fly in the fall. I am a strong believer in trigger colours for fish and it just so happens that rainbows and brookies love the colour pink.

Josh Cheater releasing a respectable white bass caught on a DDH Leech.

EASTER EGG BUGGER

MATERIALS

Designed by Stu Thompson (influenced by Russell Blessing)

Thread: Semperfli Nano Silk, 3/0, black

Hook: Daiichi 1740, size 6-12

Tail: Marabou, yellow

Body: Crystal chenille, purple

Hackle: Saddle hackle, yellow

Bead: Gold bead to suit hook size

1. De-barb the hook and slide the bead to the eye of the hook.
2. Place the hook in the vice and start the thread behind the bead, wrapping back to the point of the barb.
3. Tie in a yellow marabou feather long enough to go from behind the bead to 2 times the shank of the hook past the bend.
4. Secure the whole shaft of the feather to the hook shank by running the thread to the bead and then back to the point of the barb.
5. Eliminate the short fuzzy fibres from the feather, then tie in a yellow saddle hackle.
6. Tie in the purple crystal chenille and wrap the thread to the back of the bead.
7. Advance the chenille and tie off once the back of the bead is reached.
8. Palmer the hackle forward 5 to 6 times to form a segmented body and tie off.
9. Form the head and whip finish.

STU'S TIP What can one say about the Woolly Bugger? Catches fish no matter where you go and no matter how you fish it. In my opinion, it is the number one fly in the world and one worth having here. There are a limitless number of colour variations to this fly, but this colour combination has been my number one for a host of different fish. I can fish this pattern in so many ways, it is unreal. My preferred method is using a sink tip and drifting it along current seams in a river situation. Here is what I have caught on this pattern so far: pike, walleye, sauger, smallmouth, largemouth, white and rock bass, rainbows, browns, brookies, splake, tigers, perch, goldeye, mooneye, big mouth buffalo, carp, lake trout, channel cats, and freshwater drum. It is especially deadly for walleye.

THE SAWICH KILLER

MATERIALS — *Designed by Stu Thompson*

Thread: Semperfli Nano Silk, 3/0, white

Hook: Daiichi 2151, size 2

Tail: Polar dub, yellow (on bottom) and orange (on top)

Body: Polar dub, yellow

Wing: Polar dub, orange

Head: Polar dub, orange

1. Place the hook in the vice and start the thread at the eye of the hook. Wrap the thread back to the point of the barb.
2. Tie in a clump of yellow polar dub and then a clump of orange on top of the yellow.
3. Form a dubbing loop by letting out approximately 8 in (20 cm) of thread. Place the twister in the middle of the thread and fold back to the hook shank.
4. Secure the loop with thread wraps and advance it to the halfway point of the shank. Place the loop towards the back of the hook; you will use it shortly.
5. Tie in another clump of orange polar dub for a mid-wing.
6. Wrap the thread towards the eye stopping, approximately 1/4 in (6 mm) from the eye.
7. Pick up the dubbing loop, place the yellow polar dub crosswise into the loop, and twist tight.
8. Wet the mid-wing, stand it up straight, and wrap the dubbing noodle of yellow polar dub around the hook stopping right behind the wing.
9. Once this point is reached, push the wing down on the body and continue to wrap the noodle forward.
10. Once the thread is reached tie off the dubbing noodle and add another wing of orange polar dub.
11. Form another dubbing loop, place some orange polar dub crosswise in the loop, and twist tight.
12. Wrap the dubbing noodle 2 to 3 times to form a head and tie off.
13. Form a thread head and whip finish.
14. To apply the eyes, run a bead of Goop around the thread head, then place a dollop of Goop on the back of eyes, and press into place.
15. Wet your index finger (bowl of water beside you) and smooth out the Goop. Place the fly in a piece of foam and allow to dry.

STU'S TIP This pattern I use during autumn. I have found that fish have a trigger colour and when it is used at the proper time it is amazing fishing. The species of fish that I pursue at this time of year are brown trout and walleye. Through my experience, the absolute best time to fish for the monsters is from the second week of September until mid-October. I will use a floating line, casting to the shoreline weed beds fishing every indentation or hole I find. The size of fish I catch would shock some people—can you imagine up to 29-in (73 cm) browns and walleyes to 30 in (76 cm). Wow!

A typical fall-time brown. This fish taped out at 26 in (66 cm), according to my log. Not only did I catch this one, but I had another eight big browns that day from 21 3/4 in (55 cm) up to this one. Another unbelievable day on the water.

CLARET TIGER LEECH

MATERIALS

Designed by Ken Sawich

Thread: Semperfli Nano Silk, 6/0, black

Hook: Daiichi 2151, size 4-8

Tail: Marabou, claret with olive on top, plus 10 strands of Krystal Flash: 5 each copper and bright green

Body: Dubbing blend of gold, brown, and olive mixed by hand (may use any dubbing desired)

Under-wing: Grizzly hackle, orange

Over-wing: Grizzly hackle, orange

Bead: Glass or metal, orange

1. De-barb the hook and slide the bead up to the hook eye.
2. Place the hook in the vice. Start the thread behind the bead and wrap back to the point of the barb.
3. Tie in 5 strands of each colour of Krystal Flash.
4. Tie in the claret marabou, then add olive on top.
5. Let out approximately 6 in (15 cm) of thread and apply the dubbing mixture to it to form a noodle.
6. Take the dubbing twister and place it in the middle. Fold the thread back to the hook shank and secure the loop with a few wraps of thread.
7. Twist tight and then wrap the noodle to the back of the bead.
8. Invert the fly, pick the grizzly hackle, and place it flat along the hook shank.
9. Put the fly right-side up and repeat the previous process. Make sure the hackle goes on flat.
10. Whip finish and the fly is complete.

KEN'S TIP "I have fished this fly around the shoals in deeper water and has had tremendous success with it on some lakes on the western side of the province (Manitoba) for trout. Although I have only used this pattern for trout, I am confident that it will be an extraordinary fly for other species".

MYMINNOW

MATERIALS

Designed by Stu Thompson

Thread: Semperfli Nano Silk, 3/0, black

Hook: Daiichi 1710, size 2-8

Tail: Craft fur, grey with black bars

Body: Craft fur, grey with black bars blended with gold holographic flash

Underwing: Craft fur, white

Eyes: 1/4 in (6 mm), silver with black pupil

1. Place the hook in the vice and start the thread. Wrap the thread back to the point of the barb.
2. Tie in a tail of craft fur.
3. After securing the tail, form a dubbing loop by letting out approximately 8 in (20 cm) of thread.
4. Place the dubbing twister in the middle of the thread and fold it back towards the hook shank.
5. Wrap the thread around the shank, securing the loop then advance the thread to within 1/4 in (6 mm) of the eye.
6. Take the dubbing mixture, place it crosswise into the dubbing loop, and spin tight.
7. Take a small battery brush and brush out the loose fibres.
8. Wrap the newly formed dubbing noodle to the point where the thread was stopped.
9. Tie off the dubbing and invert the hook.
10. Take a small bunch of white craft fur and apply it to form a bottom wing.
11. Turn the fly right-side up, form the head, then whip finish.
12. To apply the eyes, run a bead of Goop around the thread head. Place a dollop of Goop on the back of the eyes and press into place.
13. With a wet finger, smooth out the Goop (bowl of water beside you) and place the fly in a piece of foam to dry.

STU'S TIP Without a doubt this is my all-time favorite stickleback pattern. I have caught more big trout on this baitfish imitation than you can imagine. I have also used this fly on a multitude of warm-water species and have done extremely well.

DeROSE DACE

MATERIALS

Designed by Stu Thompson

Thread: Semperfli Nano Silk, 12/0, white

Hook: Daiichi 2441, size 4-2/0

Tail: Buck tail, white

Body: Mylar tinsel, silver

Wing: Buck tail, white, black, and brown

Head: Deer body hair, white, black, and brown

Eyes: 1/4 in (6 mm), gold with black pupil

1. Place the hook in the vice and start the thread a third of the way back from the eye of the hook.
2. Tie in the white buck tail, ensuring it is long enough to extend past the bend of the hook 2 times the shank length.
3. Wrap the thread back to the point of the barb with touching wraps.
4. Tie in the silver Mylar tinsel and wrap the thread forward to the first tie in point. The reason for doing this is to maintain the same body diameter throughout the fly.
5. Wrap the tinsel with touching wraps to form a smooth body and tie the tinsel off.
6. Add the first wing of white buck tail and make sure the tips equal the length of the tail.
7. Tie in the black buck tail, then the brown on top. After completing this step, build a small ramp of thread as a base for the first clump of body hair.
8. Take a generous clump of white deer body hair and comb out the underfur. Place the clump on top of the hook shank and do 2 loose wraps. Push down on the body hair and ensure it surrounds the hook shank. Pull the thread down tight and do 5 more wraps through the hair to secure it.
9. Take a small clump of black body hair and place it on top of the white. Do 2 loose wraps to hold it in place.
10. Take a small clump of brown body hair and place it on top of the black and do 2 loose wraps to hold it in place.
11. Keeping your thumb on top of the hair, pull the thread taught, then comb the hair back and do 5 wraps of thread in front of the body hair.
12. Take another clump of white body hair and hold it at a 45-degree angle to the hook shank and do 2 loose wraps of thread. As the thread is tightened, the body hair will spin around the shank.
13. Take another clump of black body hair and place it on top of the white with 2 loose wraps of thread. Then take a clump of brown body hair and place on top of the black with 2 loose wraps of thread.
14. Pull the thread tight and the hair will flare out.
15. Repeat this process until the eye of the hook is reached.
16. Trim the head to the desired shape.
17. Cut eye sockets in the deer body hair and apply a dollop of Goop into the sockets.
18. Press the eyes in and place the fly in a piece of foam to let dry.

STU'S TIP This fly can be fished at any depth for any species of fish that feed on baitfish. My most favorite way to fish this fly is on a dry line when the smallmouth are in the shallows. Casting to any fallen trees or along a weed edge will always bring resounding strikes. The key to doing this type of fishing is water temperature. When the surface temperature of the water hits 68 F (20 C), the bass will literary come out of the woodwork to nail this pattern. Nothing like having that visual experience. For trout, use a sink tip line and cast along weed edges giving the fly erratic strips. All the trout species have hit this fly when I do this. This is my second favourite way to fish this fly.

Kevin Thompson holding a 21.5-in (54-cm) tiger trout caught on a DeRose Dace.

MALLARD SB

MATERIALS — Designed by Stu Thompson

Thread: Semperfli Nano Silk, 3/0, black

Hook: Daiichi 2151, size 8 or 10

Body: Mylar tinsel, gold

Wing: Mallard breast feather

1. Place the hook in the vice and start the thread at the eye of the hook. Wrap the thread in touching wraps to just in front of the point of the barb.
2. Tie in the tinsel and wrap back to the point of the barb, then advance the thread back to the eye of the hook in touching wraps.
3. Wrap the tinsel in touching wraps to the eye of the hook and tie off.
4. Tie in the mallard breast fibres to extend past the bend of the hook by 1/4 inch (6 mm).
5. Form the head and whip finish.

STU'S TIP This easy fly has taken thousands of trout through the years. I also tie this pattern with pheasant tail and guinea fowl fibres. I find that using this fly in early spring for trout is absolutely dynamite, especially if you notice where the schools of stickleback are located in a lake. Find that spot, use this fly, and hang on. The trout go ballistic over this pattern!

Rebekka Redd hoisting a beautiful male trophy brook trout.
Photo courtesy of The New Fly Fisher

Andrew Crozier with his first fish of the evening.

BENDBACK MINNOW BLACK AND ORANGE

MATERIALS

Designed by Stu Thompson (influenced by Chico Fernandez)

Thread: Semperfli Nano Silk, 3/0, black

Hook: Eagle claw L098BP

Body: Crystal chenille, medium orange

Wing: Buck tail, orange with black buck tail on top

Eyes: 1/4 in (6 mm) silver with black pupil

1. Place the hook in the vice so the curved portion of the hook is above the vice.
2. Start the thread at the midpoint of the shank and wrap the thread to the point of the barb.
3. Tie in the crystal chenille, wrap the thread forward to the hook eye, and make a half hitch.
4. Wrap the chenille forward to the eye of the hook and tie off, making sure the chenille is secure.
5. Reverse the hook in the vice, tie in the first wing of orange buck tail, and secure.
6. Tie in the second wing of black buck tail and secure.
7. Form the head and whip finish.
8. To apply the eyes, run a bead of Goop around the head.
9. Place a small dollop of Goop on the back of the eyes and press into place.
10. Smooth the Goop with a wet finger (a bowl of water beside you).
11. Place in a piece of foam and let dry.

STU'S TIP Fishing this pattern in and around weed beds is a blast because the buck tail wing will stop the fly from getting hung up on the weeds. "Toilet bowl swirls" from pike can set your heart racing and having smallmouth blasting up out of the water is not too bad, either. The tyer can adjust the colours to whatever is productive in the waters fished.

103

WHATIZIT

MATERIALS

Designed by Stu Thompson

Thread: Semperfli Nano Silk, 6/0, black
Hook: Daiichi 1530, size 4-12
Tail: Marabou, black
Body: Rayon chenille, black
Eyes: Bead chain, medium, gold

1. Place the hook in the vice and start the thread at the eye of the hook.
2. Place the gold bead chain eyes on the hook and secure with figure-eight wraps. Wrap the thread in a circular fashion between the eyes and the shank of the hook with 4 or 5 wraps to ensure the eyes do not rotate.
3. Wrap the thread back to the point of the barb and tie in the marabou tail. The marabou has to be long enough for the stem to reach the back of the eyes and the tips have to extend past the hook bend one and a half times the length of the shank.
4. Wrap the thread to the back of the eyes to secure the marabou, then wrap back to the point of the barb.
5. Tie in the chenille, secure with several wraps of thread, and advance the thread to the eye of the hook.
6. Wrap the chenille forward with a figure-eight wrap around the eyes and tie off in front of the bead chain eyes.
7. Form the head and whip finish.

STU'S TIP This is another easy fly to tie and in a multitude of colours. I have used this pattern for just about every fish that swims in my home waters and have been successful in catching them. Freshwater drum, sauger, walleye, perch, bass, trout, channel cats, carp, and the list goes on. One of my favourite springtime flies. I have to admit, my son Stefan named this fly when he asked me, "What is it?"

ERICKSON'S CLOUSER

MATERIALS — *Designed by Steve Erickson (influenced by Bob Clouser)*

Thread: Uni-thread 6/0, flat white and fluorescent pink

Hook: Mustad 34007, size 4-6

Eyes: Fly eyes, 3/16 for size 6 and 7/32 for size 4

Tail: Polar bear hair or substitute, white

Wing: Polar bear hair, black and chartreuse, or substitute

Flash: Krystal Flash, silver (optional)

Head: White thread

1. Place the hook in the vice and add a base of white thread to the hook.
2. Bring the thread back towards the eye, stopping approximately two-thirds up the hook shank.
3. Figure-eight wrap around the eyes until secure and add a drop of Super Glue or UV resin to secure the eyes.
4. Select a suitable sized clump of white polar bear hair and remove the underfur and short fibres. Then align the tips.
5. Tie in the hair at the eye and wrap the thread to secure. Wrap the thread just behind the eyes to secure the hair behind the eyes. Do two half hitches and cut the thread.
6. Add a throat of fluorescent pink thread behind the eyes and whip finish.
7. Add UV epoxy to the wraps of thread and the polar bear hair over the eyes and cure.
8. Invert the hook in the vice and start the white thread again.
9. Select a small clump of black polar bear hair, remove the underfur, then align the tips.
10. Tie the hair in at the eye of the hook and secure.
11. If so desired, tie in 2 strands of Krystal Flash with 3 wraps of thread and then double it over to form 4 strands. Trim the flash to equal the length of hair.
12. Select a small clump of chartreuse polar bear hair, remove the underfur, and align the tips.
13. Tie in at the eye of the hook and secure the hair in place.
14. Form the head with the white thread and whip finish. Add a coat of UV epoxy and the fly is complete.

STEVE'S TIP "This pattern has been primarily used on the Red River, where it has caught channel cats, walleye, sauger, freshwater drum, white bass, pike, and goldeye. It is also a very good lake pattern for pike and smallmouth bass. The heavy eyes get the fly down into the feeding zones and once at the proper depth a short stripping action will result in strikes. This pattern is tied somewhat heavily dressed compared to the typical Clouser, due to the fact that it helps to create a disturbance and improves visibility in the murky waters of the Red River."

KEVIN'S LEECH

MATERIALS

Designed by Kevin Thompson

Thread: Semperfli Nano Silk, 6/0, black

Hook: Daiichi 1710, size 4-10

Tail: Marabou (colour of tyer's choice)

Body: Darkwater Dubbing, brown

Head: Gold bead (weight of tyer's choice)

1. Debarb the hook, apply the gold bead, and slide it into position.
2. Place the hook in the vice, start the thread behind the bead, and wrap the thread to the point of the barb.
3. Tie in the marabou, ensuring the butt ends come to the back of the bead. This is to keep the same body diameter throughout the fly. The length of tail should be one and a half times the hook shank.
4. After securing the marabou, create a dubbing noodle by twisting the dubbing in a one-directional spinning motion on the thread. After applying the dubbing, wrap the noodle around the hook shank, wrapping towards the gold bead.
5. After reaching the gold bead, whip finish and the fly is complete.

STU'S TIP My son came up with this pattern when he was 10 years old. Since that time, this fly has caught a host of fish: walleye, sauger, smallmouth, White bass, crappie, carp, channel cats, freshwater drum, pike, rainbows, browns, brookies, and more. This is one fly that truly works no matter where you are and what you are fishing for. This fly also works in the following colours: olive, light olive, black, and tan.

BONUS FLY

TOKARYK KILLER

MATERIALS

Designer unknown (a fly fisher from North Dakota), tied by Stu Thompson

Thread: Semperfli Nano Silk, 6/0, white

Hook: Daiichi 1710, size 2-14

Tail: Marabou (tyer's choice of colour)

Body: Krystal Flash (tyer's choice of colour)

Wing: Krystal Flash (tyer's choice of colour)

Head: Darkwater Dubbing, tan

1. Place the hook in the vice and start the thread at the eye of the hook and wrap back to the point of the barb.
2. Tie in a tail of marabou, making sure the butt ends will come to the eye of the hook. The tail should be one and a half times the length of the shank.
3. After securing the tail, tie in about 20 strands of Krystal Flash and advance the thread towards the eye of the hook, stopping approximately 1/8 in (3 mm) from the eye.
4. Wrap the Krystal Flash forward and when tying off make sure it is at the top of the hook shank. Wrap over the flash with the thread to form a wing.
5. Ensure the Krystal Flash is secured, then cut the flash even with the bend of the hook.
6. For the dubbing head, spin whatever colour of dubbing you prefer onto the thread and form a ball of dubbing for the head. Whip finish and the fly is complete.

STU'S TIP "Originally designed for trout, this fly is a killer for bass in the shallows. I will fish this pattern in weed beds—but with a twist. I will cast into any open pocket that I see and even if I only get two or three strips, I usually have a fish hit it. Tied in the bigger sizes, I have had pike up to 40 in (1 m) when fishing the weed beds in the same manner.

THE ABOVE SMALLMOUTH was caught on an experimental streamer I was fishing. Along the shoreline of this lake are numerous weed beds, rocky shorelines, and a ton of deadfall: three of my main areas to fish for smallmouth. I tied into this fish after casting to a tree that had fallen into the water. I usually start casting the outer extremities of the deadfall and keep on casting to the area until I have completely fished every spot possible. As I placed the fly right alongside of the tree about a foot from the shoreline, this bass came out from underneath to whack it. It pays to be persistent.

DDH LEECH

MATERIALS
Designed by Stu Thompson

Thread: Semperfli Nano Silk, 3/0, black; and size A thread, fluorescent orange

Hook: Daiichi 2151, size 4

Tail: Marabou, brown

Body: Darkwater Dubbing, brown

Eyes: Bead chain, medium, gold

1. Place the hook in the vice and start the fluorescent orange thread right next to the eye of the hook. Since this style of hook is a loop eye, wrap the thread 4–5 wraps past the end of the loop then advance the thread towards the eye by 8 wraps.

2. This is the tie in point for the bead chain eyes. On this loop-eyed hook what happens when you tie in the eyes is that they are on a flat surface, so they will not rotate around the hook. Do 10 figure-eight wraps around the bead chain eyes, then wrap the thread between the eyes and the hook shank, gradually tightening the wraps. This will secure the eyes and they will not move.

3. Whip finish the fluorescent orange thread, tie in the Nano Silk, and wrap to the point of the barb.

4. Tie in the marabou tail, making sure the butt ends of the marabou come to the back of the eyes and are secure.

5. After securing the marabou, stop the thread halfway on the hook shank and form a dubbing loop.

6. Wrap the thread to the point of the barb and then back to the eye of the hook. Place dubbing mixture crosswise in the loop and twist tight.

7. Brush out the dubbing noodle with a battery brush or Velcro brush to get any loose fibres out.

8. Wrap the noodle forward and once at the eyes, do a figure eight around them. There should be enough of the dubbing noodle left to do two more wraps behind the eyes.

9. Wrap once in front of the eyes, tie off, and whip finish.

STU'S TIP Ninety-six species of fish in 15 different countries. This fly just plain catches fish: barramundi in Australia, marble trout in Slovenia, bonefish in Hawaii, and shark in the Bahamas. No matter where it is fished, it works. Not only that, but it is easily tied. This pattern can be tied in a variety of colours. Best-producing colours are olive, brown, midnight fire black, and hot olive. My best fly ever. Please see the section, Species Taken on the DDH Leech (page 193) to see this pattern's powerful versatility. This is the fly that caught the sturgeon on page 21.

RED RIVER SHINER

MATERIALS

Designed by Stu Thompson

Thread: Semperfli Nano Silk, 3/0, black

Hook: Daiichi 2151, size 2

Tail: Diamond Brite, UV pearl

Body: Diamond Brite, UV pearl

Wing: Diamond Brite, bronze olive

Eyes: 1/4 in (6 mm), gold with black pupil

1. Place the hook in the vice, start the thread at the eye of the hook, and wrap back to the point of the barb.
2. Tie in a clump of UV pearl Diamond Brite for a tail and secure with thread wraps.
3. Form a dubbing loop by letting out approximately 6 in (15 cm) of thread. Place the dubbing twister in the middle of the thread and fold it back to the hook shank. Secure the loop with thread wraps and advance the thread to the hook eye, stopping at the end of the loop.
4. Place the UV pearl Diamond Brite crosswise in the loop and twist tight, brush out any loose fibres with a small battery brush or Velcro brush.
5. Wrap the newly formed dubbing noodle towards the hook eye, stopping at the thread. Tie off and secure.
6. Tie in a wing of bronze olive Diamond Brite and secure.
7. Form a large thread head and whip finish.
8. To apply the eyes, run a bead of Goop around the thread head. Place a drop of Goop on the back of the eyes and press into place.
9. Smooth out the Goop with a wet finger (bowl of water beside you).
10. Place the fly in a piece of foam and allow to dry.`

STU'S TIP Question: Where do you find minnows in a body of water? Think about it, wherever you find them is where you will fish this pattern. Minnows typically want warmer water with less current flow. The shallows along weed beds in lakes, back eddies, dam walls, and the back side of islands in rivers are all prime locations to find minnows. Where there are minnows, there will be fish. Easy, isn't it!

SRT STICKLEBACK

MATERIALS

Designed by Stu Thompson

Thread: Semperfli Nano Silk, 3/0, black

Hook: Daiichi 2151, size 2

Tail: Marabou, white

Body: Darkwater Dubbing, white

Wing: Pheasant rump

Throat: Darkwater Dubbing, red

Eyes: 1/4 in (6 mm), gold with black pupil

1. Place the hook in the vice, start the thread at the eye of the hook, and wrap the thread to the point of the barb.
2. Tie in a tail of white marabou. The feather stem has to be long enough to go from the eye of the hook past the bend one and a half times the length of the shank.
3. Wrap the thread back to the eye of the hook and then halfway back down the hook shank.
4. Form a dubbing loop by letting out approximately 8 in (20 cm) of thread and placing the dubbing twister in the middle of the thread. Loop the thread up to the hook, wrap back to the point of the barb, then advance the thread back towards the eye of the hook.
5. Place the dubbing mixture crosswise in the loop and twist tight. Brush out the loose fibres with a small battery brush or Velcro brush.
6. Wrap the dubbing loop to the eye and tie off. Secure with a few wraps of thread.
7. Tie in a pheasant rump feather and palmer it around the hook shank. Pull all the fibres to the top of the hook shank and secure with the thread.
8. Invert the hook in the vice and add a throat of red dubbing.
9. Reverse the fly and form the head with thread, then whip finish.
10. To apply the eye, add a bead of Goop around the thread head. Place a drop of Goop on the back of the eye and press into place. Repeat for the other eye.
11. Smooth the Goop out with a wet finger (bowl of water beside you). Let dry and the fly is finished.

STU'S TIP My son, Stefan, was sitting at the tying table with me and he picked out a couple of feathers from my supply and said, "Dad, can you tie a minnow like this?" I looked at the sample jar he was pointing to, thinking, "How can I tie a stickleback with this?" This pattern was the result and it is a killer in the springtime. Once the ice recedes and you have open water, cast this fly along the shoreline and hang on. Big rainbows and browns cruise the shoreline area looking for an easy meal.

BOU BUG

Bou Bug, Orange

MATERIALS
Designed by Stu Thompson

Thread: Semperfli Nano Silk, 3/0, black

Hook: Daiichi 2441, size 4-2/0

Tail: Marabou

Body: Chenille, medium

Wing case: Marabou, and Krystal Flash, pearl

1. Place the hook in the vice and start the thread at the eye of the hook, wrapping back to the point of the barb.
2. Select a marabou feather with the stem long enough to reach from the eye of the hook to one and a half times the shank length past the bend of the hook.
3. Tie the marabou in at the point of the barb and secure it down along the hook shank.
4. Bring the thread back to the point of the barb.
5. Tie in a wing case of Krystal Flash and secure it to the hook shank.
6. Select another marabou feather and tie the tip in, with the feather lying flat. The butt end of the feather extends past the bend of the hook.
7. Tie in the medium chenille and secure it.
8. Advance the thread to the eye of the hook.
9. Wrap the chenille to the eye of the hook and tie off.
10. Bring the marabou feather over and tie down, securing with thread wraps. Trim the excess.
11. Bring the Krystal Flash over the marabou feather, secure the flash, and trim the excess.
12. Form the head and whip finish. The fly is complete.

STU'S TIP I have tied hundreds of different colour combinations of this fly and some have out-produced others. My personal favourite colours are orange, black, and tan. In smaller sizes olive, brown, and fluorescent pink are killers for trout. Some other species caught on this fly are carp, big mouth buffalo, walleye, sauger, white bass, smallmouth and largemouth, channel cats, pike, musky, crappie, and bluegill. I love fishing this fly along drop-offs.

As you can see, this Bou Bug can be tied in a myriad of colours for all types of fish. I know friends who have used the above flies on the West Coast for steelhead and salmon and have been very successful with them. On the East Coast, they have caught Atlantic salmon. No matter where, this pattern has caught fish.

This day was unbelievable with the numbers of carp I caught on Clouser's Minnow. This fly works wonders on the Red River.

Stu Thompson caught this drum on an Erickson's Clouser: the fish was 26.5 in (67 cm) and put up a terrific fight on the fly rod.

ERICKSON'S DREAM

MATERIALS
Designed by Stu Thompson

Thread: Semperfli Nano Silk, 6/0, black

Hook: Daiichi 1710, size 2-10

Tail: Darkwater Dubbing blend, consisting of polar UV, green UV, yellow, orange, and pink synthetic dubbing

Body: Same as tail

Wing: Craft fur, brown

Eyes: 1/4 in (6 mm), silver with black pupil

1. Place the hook in the vice and start the thread at the eye of the hook, wrapping back to the point of the barb.
2. Tie in a pinch of dubbing for the tail and secure the fibers with thread wraps.
3. Wrap the thread back to the half way point on the hook shank.
4. Let approximately 8 in (20 cm) of thread out of the bobbin and place the dubbing twister in the middle of the thread. Fold the thread back up to the hook shank and wrap to the point of the barb.
5. Advance the thread to the eye of the hook, stopping approximately 1/4 inch (6mm) from the eye.
6. Place the dubbing mixture crosswise in the loop and twist tight. Brush out any loose fibers with a small battery brush or Velcro brush.
7. Wrap the dubbing noodle towards the eye of the hook and tie off at the point where the thread was stopped.
8. Tie in a wing of brown craft fur and secure with thread wraps.
9. Build up the head with thread and whip finish.
10. To place the eyes, run a bead of Goop around the thread head, then place a small dollop of Goop on the back of each eye. Press the eyes into place.
11. Wet your finger (bowl of water beside you) and smooth out the Goop.
12. Place the fly in a piece of foam and allow to dry.

STU'S TIP This streamer is a relative newcomer to my arsenal, but let me tell you, what an addition! This pattern has taken 17 species of fish so far, and I believe it will take a lot more. Fishing it in erratic strips, tight to the shoreline, (2 to 3 in / 5 to 7 cm away from the shore and in about a foot of water) is a phenomenal tactic in early spring for big browns, not to mention rainbows. Smallmouth and largemouth prefer this fly along weed edges or casting it to the pockets at the back of weed beds.

What more can one say, nature's finest canvass. Nothing compares.
Photo courtesy of The New Fly Fisher

STU'S SCULPIN

MATERIALS

Designed by Stu Thompson

Thread: Semperfli Nano Silk, 3/0, black

Hook: Daiichi 2151, size 2

Tail: Marabou, olive; and UV2 Diamond Brite dubbing, olive bronze

Wing: UV2 Diamond Brite dubbing, olive bronze

Body: Darkwater Dubbing, olive

Head: UV2 Diamond Brite dubbing, olive bronze

Eye: 1/4 in (6 mm), gold with black pupil

1. Place the hook in the vice, start the thread at the eye of the hook, and wrap back to the point of the barb.
2. Tie in a piece of olive marabou long enough for the stem of the feather to cover the whole hook shank, with the tips one and a half times the shank length past the bend of the hook.
3. Once completed, tie in a wing of dubbing over the marabou and secure the butt ends of the dubbing.
4. Wrap one-quarter of the way back and let approximately 8 in (20 cm) of thread out of the bobbin. Take the dubbing twister and place it half way down the thread.
5. Fold the thread back up to the hook shank and wrap to the point of the barb. With the dubbing twister still in the loop, place it aside and prepare for the next wing.
6. Advance the thread half way up the hook shank and tie in another wing of dubbing, ensuring the tips of the dubbing meet the tail.
7. Advance the thread to the eye of the hook, stopping where the end of the loop eye meets the shank.
8. Take the dubbing loop and place the dubbing mixture crosswise in the loop and twist tight. Brush out any loose fibres with a small battery brush or Velcro brush.
9. Before starting to wrap the dubbing noodle wet the second wing and make it stand straight up (Fig. 1). Doing this will enable the tyer to wrap the dubbing noodle with no problem.
10. When wrapping the noodle, ensure that the wraps come right behind the second wing (Fig. 2), then wrap the body material over the top of the second wing. Continue wrapping the noodle to the thread and tie off (Fig. 3).
11. Add a final wing of olive bronze Diamond Brite and then create a smaller dubbing loop. Place 3 clumps of Diamond Brite crosswise in the loop and spin tight. Brush out the loose fibres.
12. Wrap this dubbing loop to form the head then brush the fibres out with a battery brush or Velcro brush.
13. Form a thread head and whip finish.
14. To apply the eyes, run a bead of Goop around the thread head. Apply a drop of Goop to the back of each eye. Press the eyes into place.
15. Smooth out the Goop with a wet finger (bowl of water beside you).
16. Place the fly in a piece of foam and let dry.

The author with a good drum he caught on Stu's Sculpin.

FIGURE 1

FIGURE 3

FIGURE 2

STU'S TIP This fly is a workhorse. Can you imagine a 39 1/2 in (1 m) channel cat? How about a 33 1/4 in (84 cm) carp? Better yet a 28 in (71 cm) Rainbow. No wait I got it, a 21 in (53 cm) smallmouth. No? Okay a 27 3/4 in (70 cm) walleye. Not a word of a lie, that is what this pattern has taken, plus a few more different species.

My favourite place on a river to fish this pattern is along a rock rubble bottom that is found along the shoreline. It is even better if there is a foam patch located above the rock rubble bottom/ I would fish a spot like that for the whole day. Nothing like fishing the foam.

ZEKE'S NIGHTMARE

MATERIALS

Designed by Stu Thompson

Thread: Semperfli Nano Silk, 3/0, black

Hook: Daiichi 2151. size 2

Tail: Marabou, chartreuse

Tag: Copper wire

Body: Darkwater Dubbing, bright orange

Wing: Black zonker strip

Head: Darkwater Dubbing, midnight fire black

Eyes: 1/4 in (6 mm) doll's eyes, white with black pupil

1. Place the hook in the vice and start the thread at the eye of the hook and wrap back to the barb.
2. Tie in the tail of marabou, ensuring the stem of the feather goes from the eye of the hook and extends past the bend of the hook one and a half times the length of the shank.
3. Secure the marabou by wrapping the thread to the eye of the hook and back to the point of the barb.
4. Tie in a piece of copper wire and secure it with the thread, then advance the thread to the 3/4-way point of the shank.
5. Place the zonker strip on top and measure for proper length; the end of the hide should be in line with the marabou tips.
6. Separate the hair and place it into position on top of the hook shank. Wrap the copper wire 3 times around the hide and shank to secure the back of the zonker strip.
7. Flip the front portion of the zonker strip back over the bend of the hook. Keeping tension on the wire, wrap it, 3 or 4 times to the thread close to the eye. Tie off the wire and trim excess.
8. Wrap the thread to the halfway point of the shank and form a dubbing loop by letting out approximately 6 in (15 cm) of thread. Place the dubbing twister halfway down and fold the thread back towards the hook. Wrap the thread back to where the zonker strip is tied in. Then advance the thread back towards the eye of the hook.
9. Place the orange dubbing crosswise in the loop and twist tight. Brush out the loose fibres with a small battery brush or Velcro brush.
10. Wrap the dubbing noodle towards the eye stopping it approximately 1/4 inch (6 mm) from the eye and tie off.
11. Cut the top of the dubbing hair off (the hair on top of the hook shank).
12. Bring the zonker strip over and tie down with secure thread wraps.
13. Form another dubbing loop and place the midnight fire dubbing crosswise in the loop and twist tight.
14. Brush out the loose fibres and wrap to finish the head portion of the fly.
15. Build the thread head and whip finish.
16. To apply the eyes, run a bead of Goop around the thread head. Place a small dollop on the back of the eyes and press them into place.
17. With a wet finger (bowl of water beside you) smooth out the goop.
18. Place the fly in a piece of foam and let dry.

STU'S STORY The first time I showed this fly to Mike Corrigan, he cringed. "The light colour should be on the belly of the fly," he stated. I'm sure he had nightmares about it. Since his nickname is Zeke and he had nightmares about this fly, I decided to name it after him. So came Zeke's Nightmare, the fly dreams are made of.

To date, this pattern has taken 16 different species of fish. Fishing this fly in current back eddies on rivers is one of my favourite tactics. Best walleye so far is 27 3/4 in (70 cm) and the best smallmouth so far is 20 in (50 cm), not to mention the pike, musky, and trout that have been caught on it.

ABOVE PHOTO The different colour combinations are limitless. With all the various colours of marabou, rabbit zonker strips, and dubbing, you can create any combination you want to imitate bait fish or one of the brightest flies imaginable. The choice is yours, but these flies do work.

Northern pike caught on a Hillbilly Baba.

BRIGITTE'S BADASS BAITFISH

MATERIALS

Designed by Stu Thompson

Thread: Semperfli Nano Silk, 3/0, black

Hook: Daiichi 2151, size 2

Tail: Polar UV2 Diamond Brite, pearl

Body: Polar UV2 Diamond Brite, pearl

Wing: Flash, silver holographic

Gills: Lite Brite, red

Eye: 1/4 in (6 mm), gold with black pupil

1. Place the hook in the vice, start the thread at the eye of the hook, and wrap the thread to the point of the barb.
2. Tie in a tail of pearl Diamond Brite dubbing.
3. Secure the tail with the thread and wrap to the halfway point of the hook.
4. Form a dubbing loop by letting approximately 8 in (20 cm) of thread out. Place the dubbing twister halfway down the thread and fold the thread back to the hook shank. Wrap the thread back to the point of the barb and then wrap back to the eye.
5. Place the Diamond Brite dubbing crosswise into the loop and spin tight.
6. Brush out the loose fibres with a small battery brush.
7. Wrap the dubbing noodle back to the eye and tie off approximately 1/4 in (6 mm) from the eye.
8. Tie off the dubbing noodle.
9. Add a wing of silver holographic flash and secure on top of the hook shank.
10. Apply a small pinch of red Lite Brite on each side for gills. Trim if necessary.
11. Form the thread head and whip finish.
12. To apply the eyes, run a bead of Goop around the thread head. Add a small dollop of Goop to the back of the eyes and press on.
13. Smooth the Goop with a wet index finger (bowl of water beside you).
14. Place the fly in a piece of foam and allow to dry.

STU'S TIP This is basically a pike fly. When fished in the shallows along the edge of the weeds, it will bring resounding strikes. It also works well for channel cats in murky water and will even take smallmouth and largemouth at certain times of the year.

MANITOBA MATUKA

MATERIALS

Designed by Steve Erickson

Thread: UNI-Thread, 6/0, olive

Hook: MFC 7026, size 4-10

Body: Darkwater Dubbing, olive and red

Wing: Coq de Leon matched saddle feathers

Hackle: Coq de Leon saddle feather

Rib: Fine gold wire

1. Place the hook in the vice and add a thread base.
2. Add weight, if desired, with fine lead wire substitute centred on the hook shank.
3. If weight is added, cover the wraps with thread.
4. Tie in gold wire at the point of the barb.
5. Dub three-quarters of the body with olive dubbing and the remaining quarter in red.
6. Select a pair of Coq de Leon feathers from opposite sides of the cape. Measure them against the hook shank and strip one side, which will be placed against the hook.
7. Tie the feathers in at the eye of the hook and lay them back over the shank.
8. Carefully wrap the gold wire through the hackle fibres to lash the wing to the body.
9. Tie in another Coq de Leon feather for the hackle, sweep the fibres back, and make two wraps. Then tie off.
10. Form the head and whip finish. The fly is complete.

STEVE'S TIP "This pattern imitates a small baitfish and has been used effectively for rainbows, browns, and brookies. This fly can also be used for any species of fish that feed on baitfish. The best method to fish this pattern is by casting into weed beds or along the shoreline and retrieve in erratic short strips. This fly can be tied in a variety of colours to match local populations of baitfish."

ROLLED MUDDLER

MATERIALS

Designed by Stephen Jay (influenced by Tom Murray)

Thread: UNI-Thread, 6/0, black
Hook: Mustad R74, size 8-12
Tail: Mallard feather fibres
Body: Mylar tinsel, gold
Rib: Small gold wire (optional)
Wing: Mallard feather fibres
Collar: Deer body hair, natural
Bead: Bead to size, gold

1. Crimp the barb of the hook and slide the bead up to the eye of the hook.
2. Place the hook in the vice and start the thread at the back of the bead. Wrap to the point of the barb.
3. Tie in a small batch of mallard breast feather. The fibres have to go past the bend of the hook by half a shank length.
4. Wrap the thread in close touching wraps back to the point of the barb.
5. Tie in the flat Mylar tinsel with close touching wraps. Advance the thread towards the bead, stopping a good 1/4 in (6 mm) from the bead.
6. Wrap the tinsel forward, stopping at the thread and tie off the tinsel.
7. Apply another small batch of mallard breast feathers, length to equal the tail, and secure with the thread.
8. Take a clump of deer body hair and place it on top of the hook shank. Press the hair down so it encompasses the shank of the hook and do 2 loose wraps of thread.
9. Pull the thread tight and the hair will flare out.
10. Whip finish and trim the body hair to the desired shape, remembering to leave the top strands to form an over wing that equals the length of the tail.

STEPHEN'S TIP "The success of this fly is the small profile and the gold bead giving the fly a bit of a jigging action. This pattern has been deadly for still water trout on both big lakes and small ponds. It can be fished close to the weed lines or pulled through the depths when the bite wanes. For shoreline fishing, I prefer to use either a floating line or a ghost tip line, depending on the vegetation around the casting area. For deeper line, sink tips seem to work best, but I rarely leave the weeds with this fly. It is for some reason, especially effective near boat launches, much to the consternation of other anglers."

LOCKPORT STANDARD

MATERIALS
Designed by Stephen Jay

Thread: UNI-Thread, 6/0, black
Hook: Gamakatsu 02008, size 4
Body: UV polar chenille over a matching colour fly tube
Eyes: Bead chain, large
Underwing: Buck tail, white
Over-wing: Buck tail, black

1. Start by adding the tube to the tube holder on your vice.
2. Once the tube is in place, lay down a thread base and add the chenille. The chenille should be tied in at a point that is 1–2 cm from the back of the tube.
3. Bring the chenille forward up to the point where the length of your tube body and chenille is just a bit shorter than the underwing. The tube will have to be cut to length after tying this fly.
4. After tying off the chenille, tie in the bead chain eyes with figure-eight wraps and secure.
5. Choose a small clump of white buck tail and tie it in for the underwing.
6. Select a small clump of black buck tail for the over wing.
7. Whip finish after the head is complete.

STEPHEN'S TIP "The fly angler can use this fly in some still water situations, but this pattern has been proven time and again on the Red River where it has taken channel cats, carp, pike, walleye, freshwater drum, sauger, goldeye, white bass, and even crappie. This is my absolute go-to fly in the Red".

DDH EYES NATURAL GREY

MATERIALS

Designed by Stu Thompson

Thread: Semperfli Nano Silk, 3/0, black

Hook: Daiichi 2151, size 2

Tail: Marabou, natural turkey, grey

Body: Darkwater Dubbing blend same as tail and holographic flash, gold

Collar: Darkwater Dubbing, midnight fire black

Eyes: 1/4 in (6 mm), gold with black pupil

1. Place the hook in the vice, start the thread at the eye of the hook, and wrap the thread back to the point of the barb.
2. Tie in the turkey marabou. The feather has to be long enough to go from the eye to one and a half times the length of the shank past the bend.
3. Secure the marabou along the hook shank with the thread, stopping at the halfway point of the shank.
4. Let out approximately 12 in (30 cm) of thread and place the dubbing twister at the halfway point. Bring the thread up to form the loop and wrap the thread to the point of the barb and then back to the eye. Do a half hitch to hold the thread in place.
5. Place 4 clumps of marabou dubbing crosswise in the loop, then add 4 clumps of midnight fire dubbing.
6. Twist the loop tight, then brush out any loose fibres with a small battery brush or Velcro brush.
7. Start wrapping the dubbing noodle towards the eye of the hook. There should be enough dubbing to cover the hook shank.
8. Tie the noodle off and form the head with thread.
9. To apply the eyes, run a bead of Goop around the head then place a small dollop of goop on the back of the eyes and press them onto the head.
10. Wet your index finger (bowl of water beside you) and smooth the Goop out to create a smooth head.
11. Place the fly in a piece of foam and let dry.

STU'S STORY "I just don't know what it is about this natural grey colour, but let me tell you it sure does catch fish. I really started to use natural grey marabou a few years ago for the occasional fly and didn't get the results I was looking for. As a result, this colour sat on the shelf for a few years before I started tying with it again. The natural grey I was using at the time was from a guinea fowl and the fly I was using was a Stuvalution. I asked a friend to try it out for me and he came back with a report that was hard to believe. Not only did he say that it was the best stickleback imitation he has ever seen, but he was catching brown and rainbows from 25 to 28 in (63 to 71 cm) all weekend long. Some 60 fish in two days of fishing. I decided to tie something similar on a larger hook and lo and behold, this pattern was born. Fourteen species of fish so far and still counting.

A small slice of smallmouth heaven. I have taken a multitude of bass from this spot with the best being 19 3/4 in (50 cm).

A fantastic brown caught on the Battenkill River by Phil Monahan of Orvis. This fish was caught on a brown DDH Leech.
Photo courtesy of Phil Monahan

DDH EYES WHITE MINNOW

MATERIALS — Designed by Stu Thompson

Thread: Semperfli Nano Silk, 3/0, black

Hook: Daiichi 2151, size 2 or 4

Tail: Marabou, white

Body: Darkwater Dubbing, white, orange, red; Ice Dub, black

Eyes: 1/4 in (6 mm), silver with black pupil

1. Place the hook in the vice, start the thread at the eye of the hook, and wrap back to the point of the barb.
2. Tie in the tail of white marabou, ensuring the stem is long enough to go from the eye to one and a half times the body length past the bend of the hook.
3. Secure the feather down by wrapping the thread to the eye and back to the barb.
4. Form a dubbing loop by letting out approximately 8 in (20 cm) of thread and placing the dubbing twister in the middle of the thread. Fold the thread back towards the hook shank and wrap the thread back towards the eye of the hook.
5. Place 2 pinches of white, 1 pinch of orange, 1 pinch of red, and 4 pinches of black dubbing crosswise into the dubbing loop.
6. Twist tight and brush out any loose fibres with a small battery brush.
7. Wrap the newly formed dubbing noodle to the eye of the hook, stopping approximately 1/4 in (6 mm) away from the eye.
8. Tie off the noodle and form the head.
9. To apply the eyes, run a bead of Goop around the head then place a small dollop of Goop to the back of the eyes and press into place.
10. With a wet finger (bowl of water beside you) smooth out the Goop.
11. Place the fly in a piece of foam and allow to dry.

STU'S STORY This pattern is a go-to fly for baitfish imitations. No matter where I go and no matter where I fish, I can count on this fly to produce fish no matter what species. There was a night when my fly fishing club had an outing on the Red River and, as it happened, I had this fly on. I landed three channel cats in a row then a friend asked if I had another one. Well, he proceeded to catch fish, then another couple of guys asked if I had anymore ... well, long story short, the six guys who got those flies were all catching fish and out-fishing the other members three to one. Just to let you know there were 31 channel cats caught that night over 34 in (86 cm) with the biggest tapping out at 39 in (99 cm). What a night of fishing! I also tie this fly with bead chain eyes, just like the one on the cover.

Jared Fontaine with one of his first channel cat on the fly. He caught it on a DDH White Minnow.

DDH HEAD PURPLE AND PINK

MATERIALS — Designed by Stu Thompson

Thread: Semperfli Nano Silk, 3/0, black

Hook: Daiichi 2151, size 4

Tail: Marabou, pink

Body: Darkwater Dubbing, pink and purple

Eyes: Bead chain, medium gold

1. Place the hook in the vice and start the thread at the eye of the hook.
2. Tie in the eyes with 10 figure-eight wraps. Wrap the thread back to the point of the barb.
3. Tie in the tail of pink marabou and ensure it is long enough to go from behind the eyes to one and a half times the shank length past the bend of the hook.
4. Form a dubbing loop by letting out approximately 8 in (20 cm) of thread. Place the dubbing twister in the middle of the thread and fold it back towards the shank. Wrap around the shank to secure.
5. Place 4 pinches of pink and 4 pinches of purple dubbing crosswise in the loop and twist tight. Brush out any loose fibres with a small battery brush.
6. Wrap the dubbing noodle forward. The pink dubbing should end right behind the eyes and the purple will begin.
7. Do one figure-eight wrap around the eyes and two wraps right behind the eyes.
8. Bring the dubbing noodle forward to the eye and tie off.

STU'S TIP The DDH series of flies have been amazing in catching fish of any species. The stories I receive from people just astound me. Can you imagine red tail cats from Malaysia, marble trout from Slovenia, and flathead cats in Georgia? What could be next? Had a young guy from Whitehorse try out some of these flies for pink salmon and he just slayed it. You can fish this fly any way you want and it will be effective. Another hint on fishing this fly: always use a loop knot to tie it on. The movement becomes unbelievable when this is done. The fly looks like a living, breathing something that is alive when it is being retrieved.

A beautiful pink salmon caught by David Cleaver on a pink DDH.
Photo courtesy of David Cleaver

PIKE & MUSKY STREAMERS

134	CG'S MINNOW	158	SR YELLOW RED HEAD
135	HILLBILLY BABA	160	BLACK & CHARTREUSE CASPER
136	TGT STREAMER	162	MIKE'S GOLDFISH
137	BUNNY LEECH	164	RC'S PUNCH FLY
138	GREEN ZACATTACK	166	SINFIELD'S MUSKY KILLER
140	RED RIVER SCULPIN	168	SINFIELD'S ZONKER
143	P & W PIKE MUDDLER	171	TJ'S FOLLY
146	WINTER'S STORM	172	TJ'S FOLLY TWO
148	KT'S BAITFISH	174	CRAFT FUR POPSICLE
150	ZONKER MINNOW PERCH	176	KEITH'S FLATWING STREAMER
152	SUPER CISCO	177	STEVE'S SHEEP DECEIVER
156	PERCH ZACATTACK		

 Easy

 Moderate

 Difficult

PIKE AND MUSKY STREAMERS

Bigger streamers for bigger fish? At times but it doesn't matter how big the fly is if they want it they will take it.

A great looking pike that was caught on a brown DDH Leech.

CG'S MINNOW

MATERIALS — *Designed by Stu Thompson (with help from my daughter, Colleen)*

Thread: Semperfli Nano Silk, 3/0, black

Hook: Daiichi 2546, size 2-2/0

Tail: Grizzly hackle, orange

Body: Crystal chenille, orange

Wing: Grizzly hackle, orange

Eyes: 1/4 in (6 mm), silver with black pupil

1. Place the hook in the vice and start the thread at the eye of the hook and wrap back to the point of the barb.
2. Tie in a tail of grizzly hackle, one on each side of the hook. The length of the tail should be 3 times the hook shank length. Secure with thread wraps.
3. Tie in the medium orange crystal chenille and advance the thread forward, stopping 1/4 in (6 mm) from the eye.
4. Wrap the chenille to the point where the thread is stopped and tie off.
5. Tie in 4 grizzly hackles, two on each side. These hackles are to equal the length of the tail.
6. Secure the hackle and form the head.
7. To apply the eyes, run a bead of Goop around the thread head. Place a dollop of Goop on the back of the eyes and press them into place.
8. Wet your index finger (bowl of water beside you) and smooth out the Goop.
9. Place in a piece of foam and let dry.

STU'S STORY Kids are awesome when it comes to fly tying. My daughter, Colleen, came up with this fly when she was six years old and I have used it faithfully since. This has become one of my searching patterns for pike and walleye and is especially effective during late September through October. I have also experimented with tying this in an #8 or #10 size of hook and have managed to land browns, brookies, rainbows, smallmouth, sauger, perch, and white bass on it. Thanks, Colleen.

HILLBILLY BABA

MATERIALS
Designed by Stu Thompson

Thread: Semperfli Nano Silk, 3/0, black

Hook: Daiichi 2220 size 1-8

Tail: Flash, gold holographic

Body: Flash, gold holographic

Bottom wing: Craft fur, white

Top wing: Barred craft fur, sand beige

Eyes: 0.40 in (10 mm), gold with black pupil

1. Place the hook in the vice, start the thread at the eye of the hook, and wrap back to the point of the barb.
2. Tie in a tail of gold holographic flash.
3. Advance the thread halfway back to the eye of the hook and form a dubbing loop. After the dubbing loop is formed, wrap the thread to the point of the barb, securing the loop.
4. Advance the thread back towards the eye, stopping three quarters of the way to the eye.
5. Place some gold holographic flash in the dubbing loop sideways then twist it tight. Brush out the loose fibres with a battery brush or Velcro brush.
6. Wrap the dubbing to where the thread is stopped.
7. Tie off the dubbing loop and invert the fly. Cut a tuft of white craft fur and do 2 loose wraps around the material. Spread the craft fur so that it encompasses the bottom of the body and halfway up the side and secure.
8. Turn the fly right-side up and repeat the process with the barred craft fur.
9. After completing this step, form the head and whip finish.
10. Brush out the whole fly to get rid of any loose fibres.
11. Apply the eyes by putting a bead of Goop around the thread, then put a small amount on the back of the eyes, and push them into place. Smooth out the Goop with a wet finger (bowl of water beside you), allow to dry. The fly is complete.

STU'S TIP This fly was designed mainly for warm-water species such as pike, walleye, smallmouth, channel cats, and carp. It still has to be tested on big rainbows and browns. This is a favourite fly to fish along drop-offs and the edges of weed beds.

TGT STREAMER

MATERIALS

Designed by Stu Thompson

Thread: Semperfli Nano Silk, 3/0, black

Hook: Daiichi 2441, size 4-2/0

Tail: Marabou, white and buck tail, black

Body: Crosscut rabbit strip, white

Wing: Buck tail, black then brown

Eyes: 1/4 in (6 mm), gold with black pupil

1. Place the hook in the vice and start the thread at the eye of the hook and wrap back to the point of the barb.
2. Select two white marabou feathers to tie in for the tail. The length should be one and a half times the shank of the hook. The shaft of the marabou feathers must be able to reach the eye of the hook to maintain the same body diameter throughout the fly.
3. Secure the marabou feathers by wrapping the thread to the hook eye and back.
4. Select a clump of long black buck tail the same length as the marabou and tie it in on top of the marabou. Ensure the thread is wrapped back to the point of the barb.
5. Tie in the white crosscut rabbit and advance the thread halfway up the hook shank.
6. Select another clump of black buck tail and tie it in at the point of the thread. Secure the buck tail and advance the thread again to the eye of the hook.
7. Wrap the cross cut rabbit forward, lifting the middle wing of buck tail out of the way. Once the middle wing is reached, wrap the crosscut rabbit over the wing and continue forward until the thread is reached.
8. Tie off the white cross cut rabbit and secure it.
9. Choose a clump of brown buck tail long enough to reach the tips of the second wing, tie it in, and trim any excess.
10. Form the thread head.
11. To apply the eyes, run a bead of Goop around the thread head, add a small drop of Goop on the back of the eyes and press them into place.
12. With a wet finger (bowl of water beside you) smooth the Goop out to form the head. Let dry and the fly is complete.

STU'S STORY In honor of my father (I called him Pop) Thomas George Thompson, I designed this fly more than 30 years ago and have taken numerous species on it. The most memorable was when I was fishing a drop-off. I was retrieving the fly when it just stopped. I set the hook and the next thing I knew; my float tube was being dragged all over the place. Never did land the fish, but what a ride. Most fun I have ever had in a float tube.

BUNNY LEECH

MATERIALS

Designer unknown

Thread: Monocord, 3/0, fluorescent orange

Hook: Mustad 7970, size 1-2

Tail: Rabbit zonker strip

Body: Rabbit zonker strip, crosscut

1. Place the hook in the vice, start the thread at the eye of the hook, and wrap back to the point of the barb.
2. Tie in a zonker strip of rabbit for the tail 2 times the length of the shank.
3. Secure the zonker strip, then tie in the crosscut rabbit strip with the hairs pointing past the bend of the hook.
4. Advance the thread and then the crosscut strip.
5. Tie the strip off at the point where the thread ended.
6. Form the head and whip finish.

STU'S TIP I do not know who developed this pattern, so I cannot give credit where it is due. I wish I could, so to the person who did come up with this fly: thank you. This easy fly pattern can be tied in so many colours it is unbelievable. Do you want an Egg-sucking Leech? Pretty easy to do: black zonker for a tail, black crosscut halfway up the hook shank, and orange or chartreuse for the final half. Easy isn't it? I have seen people fish this pattern for virtually any fish that swims, from pike and musky to bull trout and Lakers. This is one pattern that should be in your box all the time.

GREEN ZACATTACK

MATERIALS

Designed by Stu Thompson

Thread: Semperfli Nano Silk, 3/0, black

Hook: Daiichi 2546, size 1/0-5/0

Tail: Holographic tinsel, silver, 3 to 4 strands and Icelandic sheep, chartreuse

Body: Holographic dubbing, silver (rear half); and Semperfli Extreme String, red (front half)

Wing: Icelandic sheep, green (front wing), Icelandic sheep, chartreuse (second wing)

Eyes: 1/4 in (6 mm), silver with black pupil

1. Place the hook in the vice, start the thread at the eye of the hook, and wrap it to the point of the barb.
2. Tie in 3 or 4 strands of holographic silver tinsel and secure.
3. Take a small clump of Icelandic sheep and remove the underfur. Tie in the tail, making sure the tinsel and the tips of the hair are equal
4. Form a dubbing loop by letting out approximately 8 in (20 cm) of thread. Place the dubbing twister in the middle and fold the thread back towards the hook shank. Wrap the thread around the hook shank to secure the loop.
5. Place the silver holographic dubbing crosswise in the loop and twist tight. Brush out any loose fibres with a small battery brush. Wrap the completed dubbing noodle to the halfway mark of the hook and tie off, making sure the noodle is secure.
6. Invert the hook and apply the second underwing of chartreuse Icelandic sheep. The clump has to be large enough to spread half way around the hook shank and cover the bottom half of the flash.
7. Turn the fly right-side up and apply a top wing of Icelandic sheep. Once again, the clump has to be big enough to spread around the hook shank and cover the top of the silver flash. Secure both the top and bottom wing.
8. Tie in a piece of red Extreme String and wrap forward, remembering to leave approximately 1/4 in (6 mm) for the head portion of the fly.
9. Invert the hook again and repeat the second wing procedure with the green Icelandic sheep. Ensure the wing goes halfway around the hook shank.
10. Turn the hook right-side up and do the same for the top wing, once again ensuring the hair goes halfway around the hook shank.
11. Form the head and whip finish.
12. To apply the eyes, run a bead of Goop around the thread head. Place a dollop of Goop to the back of the eyes and press them on.
13. Wet your index finger (bowl of water beside you) to smooth out the Goop.
14. Place the fly in a piece of foam and let dry.

Nick Laferriere, holding a giant laker for his guest while he was guiding at Plummer's Lodge. This laker was caught on a Pink and Purple Zacattack.
Photo courtesy of Nick Laferriere

STU'S TIP With this fly being so big and because it has natural hair, it will be like casting a wet sock, so at least a 9-weight outfit would be required to cast it. With that being said, when I want to pursue bigger game fish species a 9-weight is what I will be using. I was doing pike fly-fishing seminars at a northern lodge a few years back. The seminars were during early morning and late evening so in between I had a lot of free time to fish the area, which is exactly what I did. I wanted to see how many fish I could catch on one fly and this was the pattern that I chose. The fishing was way beyond expectations. In four days of fishing, I caught and landed 1,406 pike on this one pattern (yes, I did keep count). The fishing was so incredibly hot; a lot of people wouldn't have believed it but it is absolutely true.

Casting along the edge and into the open pockets of the weed beds was the key to my success. In fact, a couple of guests also got this fly to fish with and they had the same type of success. One angler managed two really nice pike: one was 45 3/4 in (1.16 m) and the other was 47 in (1.19 m) on the nose.

This pattern can be tied in any combination of colours to imitate any type of forage fish or in any attractor colour you would like. It has been used for pike, musky, and lake trout.

RED RIVER SCULPIN

MATERIALS

Designed by Stu Thompson

Thread: Semperfli Nano Silk, 3/0, black

Hook: Daiichi 2441, size 2-2/0

Tail: Marabou, white; and Krystal Flash, pearl

Tag: Copper wire

Body: Crosscut rabbit, white

Wing: Rabbit zonker strip, grey chinchilla

Head: Antelope hair, trimmed

Eyes: 1/4 in (6 mm), gold with black pupil

1. Place the hook in the vice, start the thread a third of the hook shank away from the eye and wrap the thread back to the point of the barb.
2. Tie in the white marabou for the tail. The length of tail should be equal to the hook shank length.
3. Tie in 5 strands of the pearl Krystal Flash on each side of the marabou and secure.
4. Tie in the copper wire.
5. Measure the zonker strip; the hair fibres should equal the length of marabou on the tail.
6. Separate the hair, place the strip on top of the hook shank, and do 3 wraps with the copper wire to secure the tail of the wing.
7. Advance the wire along the hook shank and tie off.
8. Flip the zonker strip past the bend of the hook and tie in the crosscut rabbit with the tips of the hair pointing back towards the bend of the hook.
9. Advance the thread to the point where it was first tied in.
10. Wrap the crosscut rabbit to that point and tie off.
11. Trim the hair on top of the hook shank.
12. Bring the zonker strip over and tie it down, securing it in place.
13. Tie in the first batch of antelope hair with 2 loose wraps of thread, then push the hair down around the whole shank of the hook.
14. Pull the thread tight and the hair will flare out. Do 3 or 4 more wraps through the hair to secure.
15. Continue to add antelope hair until the eye of the hook is reached.
16. Trim the antelope hair to desired shape.
17. Cut eye sockets in the hair head.
18. Apply the eyes with a dollop of Goop and press into place.
19. Place the fly in a piece of foam and let dry.
20. Colour the top of the head with a black Pantone marker.

STU'S TIP This pattern has proven itself for the past 30 years. Pike, musky, channel cat, walleye, trout, smallmouth and largemouth bass have all fallen victim to this fly. I prefer fishing this fly along drop-offs that have rock rubble or small boulders on the bottom substrate.

A nice-looking walleye caught using a Red River Sculpin.

MIKE CORRIGAN, in my opinion, is one of the best fly fishermen I know. I have met very few people who have the knowledge he has and are willing to share that knowledge. He is on pro-staff for Norvise and Silver Tip Flies, was a commercial tyer, a guide on the Bow and Elk rivers, a published author, and had his flies published in Neil Jennings's book, *Fly Patterns of Southwest Alberta and Southeast British Columbia*.

Mike has caught an amazing number of different fish species during his fly-fishing career. His annual trips to the Bahamas for bonefish, tarpon, and permit, and to New Zealand for trout, are stories that I can't wait to hear. He always comes back with mythic tales of the big ones; then he shows the pictures and I just shake my head. They are spectacular!

Musky is his new passion to pursue during the summer and he does this with a fly no longer than 5 in (12 cm). His Goldfish pattern has taken multiple numbers of musky and can easily be cast with an 8-weight rod if one so desires. The great thing about this fly pattern is it works! Period. If you like to tie the bigger flies, my hat is off to you because they can be very tiring to cast. I can't see myself fly fishing all day with an 11- or 12-weight, casting humongous flies. I can see myself casting a 9-weight rod with a smaller fly, and his pattern fits the bill. Not only have I used this fly for musky, but I have also caught walleye, pike, sauger, smallmouth, largemouth, and channel cats on it. It's a versatile fly that can be tied in any colour combination for any species of fish. Well done, Mike.

P & W PIKE MUDDLER

MATERIALS
Designed by Stu Thompson

Thread: Semperfli Nano Silk, 3/0, white

Hook: Daiichi 2546, size 2-2/0

Tail: Aquarium filter fibres or Semperfli Predator Fibers

Body: Pearl UV polar chenille

Wing: Aquarium filter fibres; or Semperfli Predator Fibers; and Krystal Flash, pearl and pink llama

Head: Deer body hair, white with pink stacked on top

Eyes: 1/4 in (6 mm), red with black pupil

1. Place the hook in the vice, start the thread one-third of the way from the eye, and wrap back to the point of the barb.
2. Tie in the tail of aquarium fibres two and a half times the length of the shank.
3. Tie in the polar UV chenille and advance the thread back to the initial tie in point.
4. Wrap the chenille to the thread and tie off.
5. Tie in the first wing of aquarium fibres, then apply the Krystal Flash on top of the fibres. Next, place a small clump of pink llama on top of the Krystal Flash and secure.
6. Take a good-sized clump of white deer body hair and comb out the underfur.
7. Apply it to the hook with 2 loose wraps of thread.
8. Push down on the hair so it will encompass the whole hook shank and pull tight on the thread. The hair will flare out. Do 3 or 4 more tight wraps through the hair.
9. Take a small clump of pink deer body hair and place it on top of the white.
10. Do 2 loose wraps, ensuring the hair does not rotate to the side, and pull down tight.
11. Comb the hair back and do 3 or 4 wraps with the thread in front of the hair.
12. Repeat this process until the eye of the hook is reached.
13. Trim the hair to the desired shape and cut eye sockets in the hair.
14. Place a dollop of Goop in the eye sockets and press in the eyes.
15. Place the fly in a piece of foam and allow to dry

STU'S TIP The Pike Muddler can be tied in a variety of colours to imitate any forage fish, or tied in attractor colours. Originally designed for pike and musky, the smaller sizes have taken bass, channel cats, and walleye. One of my favourite spots on a river to fish is a back eddy by a weed bed. If a spot like this is found, fish it with every ounce of energy you have. There will always be a fish hanging around the area feeding.

WEEDMAN'S SLIDER

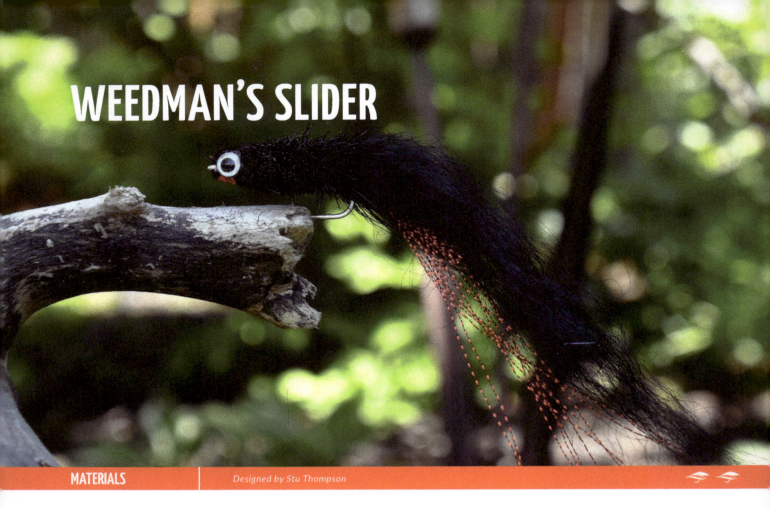

MATERIALS

Designed by Stu Thompson

Thread: Semperfli Nano Silk, 3/0, black

Hook: Daiichi 2546, size 2-3/0

Tail: Krystal Flash, red; and Icelandic sheep, black

Head: Deer body hair, black

Throat: Deer body hair, red

Eye: 1/4 in (6 mm), silver with black pupil

1. Place the hook in the vice and start the thread a 1/4 inch (6 mm) from the point of the barb.
2. Tie in the red Krystal Flash, approximately 6 in (15 cm) long, then fold the tag ends of the flash past the hook bend and secure with thread wraps.
3. Tie in a clump of black Icelandic sheep equal to the length of flash and secure the hair.
4. Take a generous amount of black deer body hair, place it on the hook shank, and do 2 loose wraps of thread around it.
5. Push the deer body hair around the hook shank then tighten the thread. Do 5 more wraps through the flared body hair.
6. Repeat this process until the eye is reached.
7. After the last clump of black body hair is completed, invert the fly in the vice.
8. Take a small clump of red body hair and place it on top of the black.
9. Do 2 loose wraps and ensure the hair is in the proper place. Pull down tight to secure.
10. Comb the hair back to expose the eye of the hook, do 6 or 7 wraps in front of the hair, and whip finish.
11. Trim the hair flat on the bottom and top, then cut the sides into a triangular shape.
12. Cut eye sockets right at the eye, apply a dollop of Goop to the socket, and press the eyes on.
13. Place the fly on a piece of foam and let dry.

STU'S TIP There is quite an origin to this pattern. I was filming an episode of *One Last Cast* with Al Carlson and during the first day I raised and hooked two musky. Being me, I forgot to bring the wire that I use for a leader. Needless to say 25-lb (11-kg) test monofilament will not work for a musky leader. Well, we got back to Al's place for an evening meal and I asked him if he had any fly-tying material. Al said he did, and pulled out the smallest box of tying material I have ever seen. It had a bag of black and red deer body hair, a bag of Icelandic sheep, and some red Krystal Flash. Anyway, I looked at the materials and it hit me. "A Dahlberg Diver," I thought, but I remembered what Al said: "We may have to go deep for them." So I sat down and started tying. First red Krystal Flash for the tail then some black Icelandic sheep. I tied the deer body hair on then thought to add a red throat. Everything checked off. I trimmed the body hair flat on the bottom and looked at the top remembering what Al said. So I trimmed the top flat as well.

"Pretty cool-looking fly," Al stated and I had to agree. We got up early the next morning with a very cold overcast day and proceeded to fish. About two hours

Mike Corrigan with a really, really nice 41-in (1-m) musky caught on his Goldfish pattern.
Photo courtesy of Mike Corrigan

later, I saw a light patch under my fly. I looked up to the sky and there was no sunshine at all so it wasn't a result of the sun. I looked back at my fly and it was still there. Then I saw a fin move and knew there was a fish following. Now I have caught and released more big fish than I care to remember, but when Al said, "Stu that fish will go over 50 inches," I lost it. I was shaking, talking in excited whispers, jumping up and down, doing everything that you were not supposed to do. The funniest moment came when the fish started to drop to the depths. As I looked down I said, "Al, the fish is sinking!" It cracked him up.

As I told this story to my manager at the time, Peter Weidman, he also cracked up so I told him I would name the fly after him so he wouldn't forget it. Hence the name Weedman's Slider. To see how well this fly works, go to my website (darkwaterdubbing.wordpress.com) and check out the videos that were supplied by *The New Fly Fisher* television show.

WINTER'S STORM

MATERIALS — Designed by Stu Thompson

Thread: Semperfli Nano Silk, 3/0, white

Hook: Daiichi 2546, size 2-4/0

Tail: Tinsel, silver; and Icelandic sheep, white

Body: Polar UV chenille

Eyes: 1/4 in (6 mm), red with black pupil

1. Place the hook in the vice, start the thread at the eye of the hook, and wrap back to the point of the barb.
2. Tie in 3 or 4 strands of tinsel for the tail approximately 6 in (15 cm) long. Add the white Icelandic sheep over top of the tinsel. Ensure all the tail fibres are secure.
3. Tie in the chenille and advance the thread to the eye of the hook. Wrap the chenille to that point and tie off.
4. Form the thread head and whip finish.
5. Run a bead of Goop around the thread head then place a small dollop of Goop on the back of the eyes.
6. Press the eyes into place, then with a wet index finger (bowl of water beside you) smooth out the Goop.
7. Place the fly in a piece of foam and let dry.

STU'S TIP Easy fly to tie? You bet. Does it catch fish? That you have to find out for yourself, but let me say this about this fly: 87. That's how many pike I caught in a day of fishing. And to top it off, over half of them were bigger than 35 in (89 cm), with the biggest topping out at 42 1/8 in (1 m). What a day, and the Winter's Storm helped make it happen. There is nothing like getting towed in a float tube while fighting big pike. Now if only I can get my flipper back!

BONUS FLY

A really nice tiger trout caught on a top water mouse called Mikey Mouse. Mike Corrigan was the angler.

KT'S BAITFISH

MATERIALS

Designed by Kevin Thompson

Thread: Semperfli Nano Silk, 3/0, black

Hook: Daiichi 2456 saltwater hook, size 2-5/0

Underwing: Icelandic sheep, white

Over-wing: Flashabou, silver; and Icelandic sheep, sky blue

Eyes: 1/4 in (6 mm), silver holographic with black pupil

1. Place the hook in the vice and start the thread at the eye of the hook.
2. Only wrap the first 1/4 in (6 mm) of the hook shank.
3. Invert the fly in the vice and apply the wing of white Icelandic sheep.
4. Turn the hook right-side up and tie in the silver Flashabou. The length should be to equal the white Icelandic sheep.
5. Tie in the blue Icelandic sheep the same length as the previous two materials.
6. Form the head with thread and whip finish.
7. To apply the eyes, run a bead of Goop around the thread head, place a small dollop of Goop on the back of the eyes, and press into place.
8. With a wet finger (bowl of water beside you), smooth out the Goop.
9. Place in a piece of foam and let dry.

STU'S STORY It is amazing what comes out of an 8-year-old's mind. This fly has taken numerous big pike and musky through the years. I have also used it for walleye, sauger, smallmouth and Largemouth bass. It has never disappointed me or my son, Kevin. One of the easiest flies to tie and the great thing is you can vary the colours to represent the different baitfish no matter where you live.

A 17-in (43-cm) white bass taken on a Red River Shiner.

ZONKER MINNOW PERCH

MATERIALS
Designed by Stu Thompson (influenced by Jim Evans)

Thread: Monocord 3/0, fluorescent orange

Hook: Daiichi 2441, size 2-2/0

Tail: Marabou, tan

Body: Crosscut rabbit, tan

Wing: Zonker strip, fire tiger

Tag: Copper wire

1. Place the hook in the vice, start the thread at the eye of the hook, and wrap back to the point of the barb.
2. Tie in the tan marabou with the feather long enough to extend from the eye of the hook to 2 times the shank of the hook past the bend.
3. Once the marabou is secure the thread must be wrapped to the point of the barb again.
4. Tie in a piece of copper wire for the tag.
5. Prepare the zonker strip and place it so the end of the hide is equal with the tips of the marabou. Separate the fibres on the strip so when it is tied in the wire will be on the hide.
6. Do 3 wraps of copper wire, lift the remaining zonker strip wing and wrap the wire towards the eye of the hook. Another 3 wraps of wire should do. Tie off the wire and trim excess.
7. With the zonker strip flipped back over the bend of the hook tie in the tan cross cut rabbit with the hair pointing to the rear of the hook.
8. Advance the thread to the eye stopping approximately 1/4 inch (6 mm) from the eye. Wrap the cross cut strip to where the thread has been stopped and tie it off.
9. Cut the top of the cross cut strip right down to the hide.
10. Bring over the zonker strip and tie down at the head and trim.
11. Form the head with thread.
12. To apply the eyes, run a bead of Goop around the head, and place a small dollop of Goop on the back of the eyes, and press them on.
13. With a wet finger (bowl of water beside you), smooth out the Goop.
14. Place the fly in a piece of foam and allow to dry.

STU'S STORY The original pattern was developed by Jim Evans of Winnipeg, Manitoba. He used a white tail and body with a black top and red throat. When Jim first tied this fly, I couldn't figure out how he got such a clean and distinct line between the crosscut rabbit and the zonker strip. After a couple of days of mulling over this fly, he finally told me the secret and was it easy. Back in 1990, Jim and I went to the FFF Conclave, where his fly was the talk of the show. I have tied this fly in a variety of colours and it has regularly produced for pike and musky. My favorite colour combination is the one that is pictured. The best pike that has been caught using this fly is 46 in (1.1 m) and the best musky is 42 in (1 m).

Craig Thomton with a massive Manitoba pike caught at Aswap Lake.
Photo courtesy of Craig Thomton

SUPER CISCO

MATERIALS

Designed by Steve Erickson

Thread: MFC Premium, 3/0, white and hot pink

Hook: Mustad 34007, size 2/0-5/0

Tail: Buck tail, white; and saddle hackle, white

Wing: Buck tail, white; saddle hackle, white; and buck tail, chartreuse

Connector: Mason Nylostrand, 20 lb wire; and 4 red glass beads

Body: Hareline Baitfish Emulator Flash, gray ghost

Throat: Buck tail, hot pink

Flash: Saltwater UV Flashabou, pearl

Head: White thread; UV epoxy; soft-body

Eyes: Tigofly 3D

1. Start with the rear section of this fly. Place the hook in the vice and wrap back to the point of the barb.
2. Add a tail of white buck tail and secure with the thread. The tail should be as long as possible without causing the buck tail to flare.
3. Add two strands of UV Flashabou to each side of the tail.
4. Apply a white saddle hackle to each side of the tail.
5. Tie in the Baitfish Emulator Flash, make 2 wraps forward, then tie off.
6. Invert the hook in the vice and tie in a bottom wing of white buck tail.
7. Turn the fly right-side up and do a wing of chartreuse buck tail on top of the hook shank.
8. Form a tapered thread head for the rear hook and whip finish.
9. Apply a coat of UV epoxy on the head.
10. Pass a length of wire leader material through the eye of the rear hook and fold over.
11. Add 3 or 4 red glass beads to the wire, passing both ends of the wire through the beads. This keeps from tangling with the fly.
12. Super Cisco Front Section
13. Pass the connecting wire through the eye of the hook and align the wire down the hook. Check that the wire is aligned to allow the rear hook to ride upright. The trailing section should sit one hook gap from the back of the front section. Tie the wire down the length of the hook. Pass the wire through the eye of the front hook, fold it back along the bottom of the shank, and lock down with thread wraps.
14. Tie in a short tail of buck tail, with white on the bottom and chartreuse on top. This tail should be short enough to not tangle in the rear hook.
15. Tie in a white saddle feather on each side of the hook.
16. Tie in the Baitfish Emulator Flash, make 2 wraps, and tie off.
17. Tie in a clump of hot pink buck tail for the throat with the hair extending just behind the hook of the front section.
18. Tie in two large clumps of buck tail with the tips facing forward. Place the white on the bottom and the chartreuse on top. Keep as much length as possible and ensure the tips are aligned. Tie in securely, up to the eye of the hook, creating a good base to tie back over. Note: The butt ends do not need to be completely covered as they will be hidden when the buck tail is folded back over the shank.

Photo courtesy of Steve Erickson

19. Tie off the white thread, add some Super Glue for strength, and allow to dry.
20. Attach the hot pink thread back from the eye where the eventual throat will be.
21. Carefully fold back the buck tail, ensuring that you get an even spread around the hook. Tie the buck tail down, pointing backwards with the hot pink thread.
22. Create a band of hot pink thread to create a hot spot on the fly and tie off.
23. Add eyes to either side of the head.
24. Coat the head liberally with soft-body and allow to dry on a fly turner. If not sufficiently covered with a single coat, repeat.

STEVE'S TIP "This was designed to be an improvement on a similar pattern that a fly fisher brought to me at Great Bear Lake, NWT. It imitates a larger cisco or small whitefish, which are some of the favoured prey of the lake trout in Great Bear Lake. It has a large profile but also moves freely because of the articulation, and the large hooks help in hooking and holding the large jaws of the lake trout there. The second hook of the articulation is helpful in hook-up rates as the trout often hit from the back. The folded buck tail head gives a great profile; however, it can be damaged easily by the fish's teeth. For this reason, covering the head with soft-body (alternatively, epoxy could be used) is helpful for producing a fly that doesn't disintegrate after four or five fish."

Does the Super Cisco work? Without a doubt. This fly can also be used for pike and musky with equal success. Steve Erickson (right) with his guest and a laker that anyone would be ecstatic about.

Photo courtesy of Steve Erickson

Kelsey Bell with one of her first channel cats; she caught eight that night, this one measuring 37 in (0.9 m), caught on a DDH Head in orange and black.

PERCH ZACATTACK

MATERIALS — Designed by Stu Thompson

Thread: Semperfli Nano Silk, 3/0, black

Hook: Daiichi 2546, size 2-4/0

Tail: Krystal Flash, pearl; and Icelandic sheep or craft fur (for smaller sizes), white

Rear body half: silver holographic flash

First underwing: Icelandic sheep or craft fur, white

First over-wing: Icelandic sheep or craft fur, yellow

Second body half: Semperfli Extreme String, red

Second underwing: Icelandic sheep or craft fur, white

Second over-wing: Icelandic sheep or craft fur, olive

Eyes: 1/4 in (6 mm), gold with black pupil

1. Place the hook in the vice, start the thread at the eye of the hook, and wrap back to the point of the barb.
2. Tie in 3 or 4 strands of pearl Krystal Flash.
3. Take a clump of Icelandic sheep and remove the underfur.
4. Place the Icelandic sheep on top of the hook and push down to encircle the hook shank. Secure with thread wraps.
5. Form a dubbing loop by letting out approximately 8 in (20 cm) of thread. Place the dubbing twister in the centre and fold the thread up back to the hook shank, wrapping the thread to secure the loop.
6. Place the silver holographic crosswise in the loop and twist tight.
7. Wrap the newly formed dubbing noodle to the halfway point on the hook shank and tie off.
8. Invert the hook in the vice, take another clump of white Icelandic sheep, push it down to cover half of the hook shank, and secure with thread wraps.
9. Turn the fly right-side up and add a wing of yellow Icelandic sheep. Once again. push the hair down to envelop half the hook shank
10. Tie in the red Extreme string and wrap it forward, leaving approximately 1/4 in (6 mm) of the shank, then tie off, and secure with thread wraps.
11. Invert the fly once again, add another underwing of white Icelandic sheep, pressing it down to cover half the hook shank.
12. Turn the fly right-side up and apply the olive sheep wing, again only going halfway around the shank.
13. Form the head and whip finish.
14. To apply the eyes, run a bead of Goop around the head, place a dollop of Goop on the back of the eyes, and press into place.
15. With a wet finger (bowl of water beside you), smooth the goop out and place the fly in a piece of foam to dry.
16. Add the black bars with a permanent felt marker.

Stu Thompson with a typical size mid summer pike.

STU'S TIP This pattern was designed specifically for big pike and musky, with the yellow perch being a basic forage fish for both species. It was easy to come up with this fly. Once all the fibres are brushed out, the silver holographic and the Extreme String will actually shine through the whole fly, giving the impression that this is a living perch. The movement of this pattern is also very life-like, whether using Icelandic sheep or craft fur. Tied in smaller sizes, this fly is dynamite for walleye and smallmouth.

The next couple of questions will give the reader something to think about. Where do you fish this fly and how deep do you fish it? I don't know if it's a sixth sense or if my dad taught me all the right things, but I always ask questions about the species of fish that I pursue, it's just ingrained in me. That said, think about where the perch are located in a river or a lake. They prefer a warmer temperature, compared to big pike. Perch prefer the water temperature to be approximately 58 F (14 C) before they start to move, and they usually move into the shallows. Big pike, in my experience, really put the feed bag on when the water temperature hits 56 to 58 F (13 to 14 C). As a result, I will try to find a shallow weedy bay at the preferred temperature for the pike because I know that the perch will be in the area looking for the warmer water. This is the case for both rivers and lakes.

Now here is something just as interesting: the preferred water temperature for perch is approximately 68 F (20 C), so I will fish this pattern until the first or second week of June with different results. Big pike, like, I said prefer 56 to 58 degrees F (13 to 14 C) and will move off to deeper water as the temperature warms, but the smaller pike will be tolerating the warmer water. So instead of catching three or four big pike, I will catch anywhere from 40 to 100 pike in a day. Granted, when the water warms, catching a pike of 30 in (76 cm) is bragging size, but with the numbers of 20- to 30-inchers (50 to 76 cm) being landed, it is a whole pile of fun.

SR YELLOW RED HEAD

MATERIALS

Designed by Stu Thompson

Thread: Semperfli Nano Silk, 3/0, red

Hook: Daiichi 2151, size 2

Wing: Craft fur, yellow, 3-4 strands Crystal flash, pearl

Head: Crosscut rabbit, red

Eyes: 1/4 in (6 mm), silver with black pupil

1. Place the hook in the vice, start the thread at the eye of the hook, and wrap one-third of the length of the shank from the eye.
2. Invert the fly in the vice and do a bottom wing of 3-4 strands of pearl crystal flash and then add the yellow craft fur, ensuring the material goes halfway around the shank.
3. Set the hook in the vice right-side up and do a top wing of yellow craft fur, once again going halfway around the hook shank.
4. To secure the wing, do a ramp of thread towards the hook eye.
5. Tie in the red crosscut rabbit where the wing is tied in. The tips of the hair should be pointed to the bend of the hook.
6. Wrap the crosscut rabbit to the eye of the hook and tie off.
7. Form the head and whip finish.
8. To apply the eyes, run a bead of Goop around the thread head. Place a dollop of Goop on the back of the eyes and press them into place.
9. Smooth out the Goop with a wet finger (bowl of water beside you).
10. Place the fly in a piece of foam and allow to dry.

STU'S TIP The one thing about tying this fly is that it is easy to do and it is a very effective fly for pike, perch, and walleye. Fishing this pattern on top of a reef or along the drop-off during early morning can produce quite a few fish. Another spot that I fish this pattern is in front of a small creek that flows into a lake, where there is just enough current flow to attract the fish. With the undulating movement of this pattern, it is a killer in these situations.

Photo courtesy of Steve Erickson

STEVE ERICKSON is a high-school teacher with a passion for fly fishing. Not only does he teach but during the summer holidays, he guides for Tree River Lodge for a month. He's one of the most knowledgeable Arctic char fly fishers around. He also has extensive knowledge about the fishing in and around the Manitoba area and has caught just about every game fish species in the province. His Sheep Deceiver is a pattern that can be used anywhere there are fish. Tied in different sizes, it can take channel cats or trout, and it is a universal pattern that has proven itself time and again. His Craft Fur Popsicle is also one of the best char flies that you can use. Arctic char, lake trout, and brook trout have all fallen victim to this pattern.

BLACK & CHARTREUSE CASPER

MATERIALS Designed by Stu Thompson

Thread: Semperfli Nano Silk, 3/0, black

Hook: Daiichi 2546, size 2-5/0

Tail: Badger hackle

Body: Crosscut rabbit, chartreuse and white

Eyes: Moveable doll's eyes

1. Place the hook in the vice, start the thread at the eye of the hook, and wrap the thread to the point of the barb.
2. Select 4 saddle hackles and tie in for the tail, two on each side. Ensure the hackle is long enough to extend from the eye of the hook past the bend, approximately 4 times the hook shank length.
3. Wrap the thread back to the eye of the hook, then wrap it back to the point of the barb.
4. Tie in the crosscut rabbit with the tips of hair pointing to the bend of the hook. Advance the thread back to the eye of the hook.
5. Wrap the crosscut rabbit to the eye of the hook and tie off.
6. Form the head with the thread and whip finish.
7. To apply the eye, run a bead of Goop around the thread head. Place a dollop of Goop and the back of the eyes and press into place.
8. Smooth the Goop out with a wet finger (bowl of water beside you).
9. Place the hook in a piece of foam and let dry.

STU'S STORY When I first started fly fishing, I was mainly pursuing pike and walleye because that is what my Dad wanted to go after. So the first few years of fly fishing was for these species, which required some problem-solving to fish the way I wanted. I had to figure out a way to effectively fish submerged weed beds, so I started looking at ways to achieve this.

It came to me one night when I looked at a goofy thing my sister made at Girl Guides; at least I thought it was goofy-looking. Anyway, this thing had moveable doll's eyes and that really got me thinking. So the first thing I tried, after buying some eyes, was to drop them in a glass of water. Bingo! They floated, which was exactly what I was looking for. Next, I tied a fly and glued on the eye with Krazy Glue. First mistake: never adjust the eyes when the Krazy Glue is still wet; glues your fingers together pretty quick. After seeing a 13-year-old running around the house screaming, "I can't get my fingers apart," my Mom took pity on me. She dried her eyes from laughing so hard and then she got out her nail polish remover and got my fingers unstuck. Moms are wonderful people, but I can tell you that nail polish remover did not leave my sight again.

Well, I got the fly finished and I wanted to see how far it would sink. Yep, filled the bath tub to check it out. The first one sank about 10 in (25 cm) and it stopped and stayed at that depth. I gave a tug on the line I tied

Not the biggest, but still a ton of fun on the fly rod.

to the fly and it moved up a short way and sank back down to the same depth. So after this experiment I was shaking the fly off and, lo and behold, I heard the rattle of the eyes. Yep, I now had a suspending fly that rattles. What a killer.

A few years later, I was a tyer at the FFF Conclave. Bob Krumm was watching me tie this pattern and was asking questions about it. One comment he made, and I had a good laugh out of it, was "You used half a chicken to tie this." Not quite, but it looked like it. Now because it was an all-white concoction with yellow and black eyes, he said, "That looks like Casper the Friendly Ghost." Little did he realize that he had named the fly. The Casper series of flies has caught big pike and musky along with smallmouth, sauger, walleye, channel cats and, on occasion, trout (of course, in smaller sizes).

One last note when using the moveable doll's eyes: when you use different sizes and different hooks you get different sink depths, so if you want a fly to only sink 6 in (15 cm), use the smallest eyes on a light wire hook. The possibilities are endless. The best colours that I have used are white, orange, black with a red head, and chartreuse and black. Another way to fish this fly is to use a full sinking fly line. What happens is the fly line will sink to the bottom but the fly will ride just above it enabling the angler the opportunity to fish for suspended fish close to the bottom.

MIKE'S GOLDFISH

MATERIALS — Designed by Mike Corrigan

Thread: Clear mono (invisible thread)

Hook: Gamakatsu SC-15 2H, size 3/0 or equivalent

Head: Mylar tubing (tied in just above the hook point)

Underwing: Acrylic yarn, light orange

Over-wing: Acrylic yarn, fluorescent orange

Eyes: 1/4 in (6 mm) 3D, silver with black pupil

How to Card* Acrylic Yarn (see page 190)

1. Cut 10 strands of 100% acrylic yarn and knot all of them together. Place the knot in the middle of the yarn and pull tight. Take the yarn, and using a self-healing cutting board, comb with a dog brush. Start with the tips of the yarn on one side of the knot and work your way towards the knot until all the yarn is fluffy. Do the same for the other side of the yarn.

2. Place the hook in the vice and position the Mylar tubing by sliding it over the eye of the hook to the bend

3. Attach the thread, bind the rear of the tubing to the shank of the hook, add a drop of Krazy Glue, and cut the thread.

4. Push the Mylar back towards the bend of the hook so it forms a cup facing the rear of the hook. Reattach the thread and bind down the front of the Mylar tubing. Cut the excess Mylar off and add another drop of Krazy Glue. The finished tubing should ideally be located in the back third or half of the shank of the hook. Figure 1.

5. Using the fluorescent orange yarn, tie it on top of the shank over the front of the Mylar with the tapered end over the eye of the hook (also known as reverse tying).

6. Tie it in before cutting it off at the knot and add a drop of Krazy Glue.

7. Rotate the hook in the vice and repeat the previous step with the other colour of yarn. While the hook is still upside down, take this second clump of yarn, divide it in half, and pull it at right angles to the hook shank. Again add a few drops of Krazy Glue, tie a couple of half hitches, and cut the thread.

8. Grab all the clumps of yarn and pull towards the rear of the hook. Use a comb to blend the yarn together.

9. Hold the yarn on top of the vice with a hair clip.

10. Add the eyes using Krazy Glue Gel and the fly is complete.

11. Flash can be added if so desired.

162

Figure 1

✱CARDING NOTES With the acrylic yarn, the maximum length of the fly is 4 to 5 inches (12 to 15cm). The fly tends to foul more if you tie the yarn near the eye of the hook. If the fly does foul, just work the fibres into their original configuration, keeping in mind that the bottom piece of yarn is split 50-50 along the sides of the fly. The two tones of orange will help guide where the fibres belong. The fly is remarkably durable with the eyes being the most vulnerable. Other adhesives may keep the eyes affixed longer, but they drastically change the fly's movement. When the fly does get trashed (from all the fish), just cut off everything except the Mylar and retie it.

MIKE'S TIPS "The Goldfish has accounted for over 90 percent of the musky I have caught. It also works well on tarpon, pike, and bass. The following colours have worked extremely well for the above species: orange, chartreuse and white, black and purple, pink, and red and white. I have taken trout on smaller versions, (size 8-12 hooks) in the following colours: tan, olive, and greys."

RAIN DROP

MATERIALS

Designed by Stu Thompson

Thread: Semperfli Nano Silk white 3/0

Hook: Daiichi 2546 size 2/0-5/0

Tail: Semperfli Predator fibers white and crystal flash pearl

Body: Semperfli extreme string fl. silver

Gills: Semperfli extreme string red

Wing: Semperfli Predator fibers white

Over wing: Senyo's UV barred Predator wrap

Eyes: 6mm (1//4in) gold with black pupil

1. Place the hook in the vise and start the thread at the eye of the hook and wrap back to the point of the barb.
2. Tie in 3 or 4 strands of crystal flash.
3. Select a small clump of white Predator fibers and place on top of the hook.
4. Press the fibers down to surround the hook shank and secure with the thread.
5. Tie in the fl. silver extreme string and wrap it forward towards the eye stopping approximately three quarters of the way up the hook shank.
6. Tie off the silver and tie in the red extreme string to make the gills. Wrap this material until it is 1/4 inch (6mm) from the eye of the hook and tie off.
7. Invert the hook in the vise and apply some more white Predator fiber to form a bottom wing around half the hook shank.
8. Turn the fly right side up and repeat this step for the over wing.
9. Tie in the Senyo's UV Predator wrap and do two complete turns and tie off.
10. Form the head and whip finish.
11. To apply the eyes run a bead of goop around the thread head and place a dollop of Goop on the back of the eyes. Press into place.
12. Smooth out the Goop with a wet finger. (bowl of water beside you)
13. Place in a piece of foam and allow to dry

Fellow fly fisherman, John Veenstra, with his personal best Musky sitting at 41 inches (1meter). Awesome job John.
Photo courtesy of Mike Corrigan

STU'S STORY This is a fun pattern to fish not only for Pike and Musky but there are some suicidal Smallmouth that will absolutely smash the tar out of it. For Pike I have found some really great river mouths that I fish. What I will usually do is travel up the river about one mile, if possible, and take my time fishing all the way back to the mouth. Depending on the weed growth I will cast the fly within a foot of the shore and strip it out toward open water. It is super fun watching 7 or 8 bow waves coming after your fly and when they hit the fly it is like being on a sugar high for days. Your hands are shaking and it's all you can do to focus for another cast. I have a blast fishing like this. Musky are another animal all together but I will do the same technique around the weed beds, cast shallow and retrieve to deeper water. Gets your heart beating when you get a Musky hitting or following your fly especially in a float tube. Yikes!

RC'S PUNCH FLY

MATERIALS

Designed by Stu Thompson (influenced by Dan Blanton)

Thread: Semperfli Nano Silk, 3/0, black

Hook: Daiichi 2546, size 2-5/0

Tail: Buck tail, white; and Krystal Flash, red

Body: Mylar tinsel, silver

Wing: Peacock herl and grizzly hackle

Throat: Hackle, red

Head: Ultra chenille, white medium

Wing Case: Peacock herl

Eyes: Fly eyes 7/32, yellow with black pupil

1. Place the hook in the vice and start the thread at the eye of the hook.
2. Attach the eyes to the bottom of the hook shank with figure-eight wraps and, if desired, apply a drop of Krazy Glue to secure.
3. Select a clump of buck tail and tie it in behind the eyes. The buck tail should start at the back of the eyes and go three times the hook shank length past the bend. Add the Krystal Flash.
4. In close-touching wraps, take the thread to the point of the hook and tie in the tinsel.
5. Wrap the thread back to the point of the barb then advance the thread back towards the eye of the hook, stopping two-thirds of the way up the hook shank.
6. Wrap the tinsel in touching wraps to the thread and tie off.
7. Tie in the red hackle and do 3 wraps. The length of hackle fibres has to reach the bend of the hook.
8. Push the hackle down so all of it is underneath the hook shank and secure with thread wraps.
9. Tie in a wing of peacock herl to equal the length of buck tail.
10. Tie in a grizzly saddle hackle along each side. The hackle is not trimmed, keeping the marabou part of the feather intact. The length of this wing equals the length of buck tail.
11. Take approximately 15 strands of peacock herl and fold them in half. Tie this bundle in to form a wing-case for the head.
12. Tie in a piece of ultra-chenille and wrap the thread to the eye of the hook.
13. Wrap the chenille to form the head, with a figure-eight wrap around the eye.
14. Tie off the chenille and secure. Pull the peacock herl over the chenille and tie down.
15. Form the thread head and whip finish.

The wicked teeth of a top-of-the-line predator.
Photo courtesy of Mike Corrigan

STU'S STORY I met Dan Blanton at the second Federation of Fly Fishers Conclave that I attended. What I noticed most about the flies he was tying was the size of them and the way they were tied. His Punch Fly series just screamed BIG PIKE! So I sat in front of him and asked if he could tie one of the Punch Flies. As he was showing me the pattern, it dawned on me that I knew all the techniques but I never put them in the order he did. What a wakeup call. The next year, I went to find him to show him what I tied and he was suitably impressed. I also asked if I could name the fly RC's Punch Fly and he said, "Absolutely." So for the last 39 years, this pattern has been catching fish. My best pike on it so far is 44 in (1.1 m) and my best musky is 41 in (1 m). But here is the cool thing about this fly: in smaller sizes it has taken 20 different species of fish. A really great all around streamer pattern for fresh and salt water.

SINFIELD'S MUSKY KILLER

MATERIALS — Designed by Keith Sinfield (influenced by Andy Sobota's "Swimmy Jimmy")

Thread: UTC 140D and Veevus Power 140 (for spinning deer body hair)

Hook: Daiichi 1710, size 4; and Mustad C52S BLN, size 1/0

Body: Marabou, white; and Flashabou, pearl

Wing: Marabou, olive

Head: Deer body hair, olive and white

Eyes: 1/4 in (6 mm), red with black pupil

Connection: 0.024 Beadalon wire; and 2 white beads

1. Place the Daiichi hook in the vice, start the thread at the eye of the hook, and wrap back to the barb.
2. Tie in the first white marabou feather by the stem and wrap it forward.
3. After tying off at the tip of the feather, comb all the fibres back and wrap the thread 3 to 4 times to secure. Repeat this procedure until you are within 1/8 inch (3 mm) of the eye of the hook.
4. If flash is required, tie in two strands of Flashabou on each side.
5. Tie in an olive marabou feather for the dark wing.
6. Form a small head and remove the hook from the vice.
7. Place the Mustad hook in the vice after putting a 25-degree bend at the halfway point of the shank. Start the thread at the eye of the hook and wrap back to the point of the barb.
8. Take the wire and loop it through the rear hook that is completed. Place the beads on the wire, ensuring the beads cover both strands. Adjust the loop to the size required.
9. Place the wire on the hook and secure it with thread wraps. Note: The wire loop has to be perpendicular to the front hook in order for the fly to swim correctly.
10. Wrap the thread back to the point of the barb and tie in a white marabou feather by the stem.
11. Palmer the marabou forward and tie off the tip. Comb all the fibres back and secure with 3 to 4 wraps of thread.
12. Continue this procedure until the midway point of the shank is covered with the marabou.
13. Add 2 strands of pearl Flashabou on each side.
14. Tie in the olive marabou feather to create the dark wing.
15. Tie off the UTC thread and tie in the Veevus thread to apply the deer body hair.
16. Take a clump of olive deer body hair and place on top of the hook shank. Do 2 loose wraps, hold the body hair on top of the hook shank, and pull the thread tight. Do 2 or 3 more wraps through the hair to secure.
17. Invert the fly in the vice and repeat the procedure for the white deer body hair.
18. Repeat the process until the eye is reached.
19. Trim the hair to the desired shape and cut an eye socket on each side of the head.
20. Place a dollop of Goop in the eye sockets and press on the eyes.
21. Place the fly in the foam and let dry.

Releasing a 22-in (55-cm) smallmouth.

KEITH'S TIP The fly should float to the surface when paused on the retrieve and dive down when stripped in. When imitating a struggling baitfish, the angler has to have an erratic retrieve with a number of pauses. To fish this pattern deeper, use a sink tip or a full sink line. Colour combinations that work well are olive and white, chartreuse and white, red and white, and tan and white. This fly can be in a larger size for bigger musky and pike but can also be downsized to fish trout and bass.

SINFIELD'S ZONKER

MATERIALS — Designed by Keith Sinfield

Thread: UTC 140D, orange
Hook: Togen SS18428, size 1/0
Body: UNI Mylar, #12 pearl
Tail: Craft fur, white; and 2 saddle hackles, white
Rib: Gold wire, small
Wing: 2 Zonker strips, white
Throat: Rabbit hair, orange
Eyes: 3/16 (x mm) fly eyes
Flash: Flashabou 2 strands, pearl

1. Place the hook in the vice and start the thread at the eye of the hook.
2. Tie in the dumbbell eyes, about 1/4 inch (6 mm) from the hook eye, with figure-eight wraps. Wrap the thread to the point of the barb with touching turns.
3. Tie in a generous clump of white craft fur. After removing the underfur, the tail should be 2 1/2 in (6 cm) long.
4. Trim off the excess fur at the tie in point and apply the two white saddles, one on each side, to equal the length of the craft fur.
5. Cut off the shafts of the feathers just behind the eyes and wrap the thread forward finishing right behind the eyes.
6. Tie in the ribbing and wrap the thread back to the tail in close wraps.
7. Tie in 2 strands of pearl Flashabou on each side of the tail. Tie in the Mylar tinsel and advance the thread to just behind the eyes.
8. Add a thin coat of head cement to the thread body then wrap the Mylar forward in touching wraps. Tie off the Mylar right behind the eyes.
9. Tie in the first zonker strip just in front of the eyes. Once secure, do a couple of figure-eight wraps around the eyes to secure.
10. Holding the zonker strip straight out and on top of the hook shank, wrap the ribbing wire forward to the eyes. Secure the wire and trim the excess. The length of zonker strip should be three-quarters the length of the tail.
11. Take a generous clump of orange rabbit fur and tie in front of the eyes to form the beard.
12. Attach the second zonker strip in front of the eyes and wrap the thread back to hold the zonker strip tight to the front of the eyes.
13. Lift the zonker strip up and add a drop of Super Glue to the top of the dumbbell eyes. Press the top of the zonker strip down onto the glue. The rest of the zonker strip will be loose. The length of the second zonker strip is three-quarters the length of the first strip.
14. Form the head of the fly and coat with a UV clear coat or lacquer of choice.

KEITH'S STORY "I do not know who the originator of this fly is, but I have tied this pattern with a variety of tails. Some with synthetic material, some with slight variations of natural hairs instead of craft fur. The head remains the same. The fly has worked extremely well on lake trout, pike, bass, and walleye. The weight will get the fly down to the proper depth and the placement of the eyes will give it less of a jigging motion when stripped in."

A Rock bass of epic proportions, this one taped out at 12 in (30.48 cm), caught by my son Kevin on, what else, Kevin's Leech

Marcel Duval of Winnipeg holds a pike from the Red River.

TJ'S FOLLY

MATERIALS

Designed by Stu Thompson

Thread: Semperfli Nano Silk, 3/0, white

Hook: C. G. Emery Kamakazi #11716, size 2/0

Tail: Hends angel hair, gold and metallic brown

Head: Buildup of Nano Silk, coloured with a brown felt marker

Eyes: 1/4 in (6 mm), silver with black pupil

1. Place the hook in the vice, start the thread at the point of the hook, and wrap back to the point of the barb.
2. Tie in the first clump of gold angel hair.
3. Take a clump of brown angel hair and tie it on top of the gold.
4. Form a large head with the thread covering the last one-third of the hook shank.
5. Add the eyes by placing a bead of Goop around the thread head.
6. Place a dollop of Goop on the back of the eyes and press them into place.
7. Smooth out the Goop with a wet index finger (bowl of water to your side).
8. Place into a piece of foam and allow to dry.
9. To make this pattern more durable the tyer may use epoxy to coat the thread head and eyes.

STU'S TIP I just love to fish patterns like this; not too much to them but boy do they catch fish. Tons of pike with quite a few musky thrown in for good measure. Not only that, but there are some kamikaze bass out there that think there is nothing better than smacking this fly. A great producing pattern, no matter how it is fished.

TJ'S FOLLY TWO

MATERIALS
Designed by Stu Thompson

Thread: Monocord, 3/0, fluorescent pink

Hook: C. G. Emery Kamakazi 11716, size 2/0

Tail: Hends angel hair, pink pearl and black

Collar: Darkwater Dubbing, midnight fire black

Eyes: 1/4 in (6 mm), silver with black pupil

1. Place the hook in the vice, start the thread at the hook point, and wrap the thread back to the point of the barb.
2. Tie in the pink angel hair.
3. Next, apply the black angel hair on top of the pink.
4. After securing the tail form a dubbing loop, letting approximately 6 in (15 cm) of thread out of the bobbin.
5. Place the dubbing twister in the middle and fold the thread back to the hook shank. Secure with thread wraps.
6. Place the Darkwater Dubbing crosswise into the loop and twist tight. Brush out any loose fibres with a small battery brush.
7. Do 3 wraps of the dubbing noodle and tie off.
8. Create the head by wrapping the thread.
9. To apply the eyes, run a bead of Goop around the thread. Place a dollop of Goop on the back of the eyes and press into place.
10. Smooth out the Goop with a wet finger (bowl of water beside you).

STU'S TIP At the tyer's choice, a coat of epoxy may be applied. This will make an indestructible fly. Once again, this pattern was designed for pike and musky but where you have these fish there are always other species in the water as well. Smallmouth, walleye, and sauger have all fallen victim to this fly. Dry lines and weed beds and I'm a happy man!

The author with an impressive 25 1/2-inch (64-cm) brown trout taken at a lake in the Parklands area of Manitoba.

CRAFT FUR POPSICLE

Photo courtesy of Steve Erickson

MATERIALS

Designed by Steve Erickson

Thread: Semperfli Nano Silk, 3/0, black and white

Shank: Fish skull, 1-in (35-mm) articulated shank

Connector: Mustad Fastach clip, size 1

Hook: Gamakatsu 02009 octopus hook, size 2

Eyes: Fly eyes 7/32; and Tigofly 3D eyes

Tail: Marabou, white

Body: UV Ice Dub, white

Rib: Silver wire, fine

Underwing: Craft fur, white

Wing: Marabou, white and black

Throat: Schlappen, red

Flash: Flashabou, multicolour

Head: Darkwater Dubbing, black

1. Place the Fish Skull shank in the vice and start the thread at the eye.
2. Using the black thread, attach the eyes to the shank with figure-eight wraps. Leave enough room to dub around the eyes and form the head.
3. Switch to the white thread and cover the hook shank. Before closing the loop at the back of the shank, place a Fastach connector onto the shank loop by the closed loop end of the connector, leaving the quick connection end available for the hook.
4. Complete the thread base to the rear of the shank, closing the loop.
5. Tie in a white marabou feather by the tip and wrap it on as a tail, popsicle-style.
6. Add 6 strands of Flashabou to the tail and spread it around the fly.
7. Tie in the wire for the rib.
8. Create a dubbing loop by letting out approximately 8 in (20 cm) of thread and placing the dubbing twister in the middle of the thread. Fold the thread back towards the hook shank and wrap the thread around it to secure the loop.
9. Take the UV ice dub and place it crosswise in the loop and twist tight. Brush out any loose fibres with a small battery brush.
10. Advance the thread towards the eye of the shank and stop approximately 1/2 in (1 cm) from the eye.
11. Wrap the dubbing noodle to the point where the thread is and tie off.
12. Wrap the rib forward in 6 evenly spaced wraps and tie it off.
13. Create another dubbing loop, cut a section of craft fur (removing the short fibres), then place the craft fur in the loop, supported on a piece of paper, so the tips are all free and the butts in the loop.
14. Carefully spin the loop to catch all the butt ends, being careful not to catch the tips.
15. Wrap the craft fur dubbing around the hook, brushing the fibres back ensuring all the tips point backwards.
16. Tie in a white marabou feather and wrap it over the craft fur, popsicle-style.
17. Tie in a black marabou feather and repeat the above process.
18. Whip finish the white thread and start the black thread.
19. Tie in the red Schlappen and wrap it as a collar over the black marabou.

176

Phil Monahan, who writes The Orvis Fly Fishing Blog, with a beautiful marble trout caught on the Soca River in Slovenia. He was using an olive DDH Leech.

Photo courtesy of Phil Monahan

20. Create a dubbing noodle by letting out approximately 5 inches (12 cm) of thread and with a spinning motion apply the black dubbing.
21. Wrap the dubbing around the eyes, creating the head.
22. Create the thread head and whip finish. Coat the head with UV head epoxy.

STEVE'S TIP "The craft fur collar keeps the marabou from collapsing onto the hook, giving this pattern a fuller profile compared to a typical popsicle style fly, while retaining the movement of the marabou. The Fastach connector is an easy way to allow for changing the hook, if so desired. This fly has been a consistent producer for pike and lake trout, and I have no doubt it will take a myriad of fish".

KEITH'S FLATWING STREAMER

MATERIALS   Designed by Keith Sinfield

Thread: UTC 140D, white

Hook: Togen SS18428, size 4

Tail: Craft fur, chartreuse; 2 grizzly hackles; and 2 strands Flashabou, pearl

Body: Hareline Crystal chenille, medium, shrimp pink

Over-wing: Craft fur, grey

Underwing: Craft fur, white

Eyes: 1/4 in (6 mm) 3D, silver with black pupil

1. Place the hook in the vice, start the thread at the hook eye, and wrap back to the point of the barb.
2. Tie in a clump of chartreuse craft fur at the point of the barb. Cut off excess and create a slight ramp of thread.
3. Tie in the grizzly hackle, one on each side, so the tips of the feather equal the length of the craft fur. The shafts of the feathers must be able to reach the eye.
4. Wrap the thread to the eye of the hook and then wrap back to the point of the barb.
5. Tie in two strands of pearl Flashabou on each side of the tail.
6. Apply the crystal chenille and secure into place at the point of the barb and advance the thread to within 3/16 in (4 mm) of the eye.
7. Wrap the chenille to the eye of the hook, stopping and tying off at the thread location.
8. Invert the fly in the vice and add the underwing of white craft fur, ensuring that the fur encompasses the bottom half of the hook shank.
9. Turn the fly right-side up in the vice and apply the grey craft fur on the top half of the hook shank. Secure the craft fur and form the head with the thread.
10. Use a drop of Krazy Glue for each eye and press into place.
11. Let dry and then coat the head and eyes with a UV coating.

KEITH'S TIP "A great pattern for pike, walleye, bass, and lake trout. When fishing on lakes, especially eastern Manitoba, or western Ontario, look for a granite shoreline that falls directly into the water. There are always drop offs along this type of shoreline and if there is a weed bed on one end of the drop off fish it as hard as you can. I always find big fish in these areas. Tied in a smaller size, it would be ideal for the trout species. Intermittent quick strips with pauses will entice a predator's response."

STEVE'S SHEEP DECEIVER

MATERIALS

Designed by Steve Erickson

Thread: MFC Premium, 3/0, white

Hook: Mustad 34007, size 2-2/0

Tail: Icelandic sheep, white

Body: Silver braid

Throat: Icelandic sheep, white

Wing: Icelandic sheep, black over red

Flash: Flashabou, UV pearl

Eyes: Tigofly 3D eyes

1. Place the hook in the vice, start the thread at the eye of the hook, and wrap the thread back to the point of the barb.
2. Tie in a tail of Icelandic sheep. The hair should extend from the last three-quarters of the shank to two times the length of the hook past the bend.
3. Tie in 4 to 6 strands of Flashabou on each side of the tail.
4. Tie in the silver braid and advance the thread to the end of the hair.
5. Wrap the braid body with close touching wraps and tie off.
6. Invert the hook in the vice and add a clump of white Icelandic sheep for a throat. The length should be equal to the tail.
7. Turn the fly right-side up and tie in 8 strands of pearl Flashabou.
8. Tie in the red Icelandic sheep and add the black on top.
9. Form the head and apply stick-on eyes.
10. Coat the head with epoxy and allow to dry.

STEVE'S TIP "This was designed to be a very simple tie representing a cisco or other forage fish. The deceiver calls for feathers and buck tail, so replacing these with Icelandic sheep simplifies the pattern, and the long wool moves like it is alive in the water. This pattern is very effective for lake trout and pike but adaptable to colours to match baitfish anywhere."

STEPHEN JAY is one of the most accomplished fly fishermen that I know. He loves to fish rivers, especially for trout, and in Manitoba that is a little hard to find. So he does the next best thing: he fly fishes the Red River. Of course there are no trout located in this body of water, but he has proven to everybody that warm-water species can be readily caught on the fly. In fact, one of his favourite patterns to use on the Red is a Prince Nymph. With this fly, he has caught some freshwater drum, walleye, sauger, crappie, white bass, carp, and channel cat. Impressive when you consider this was done with a trout fly! His Lockport Standard tube fly is one of the best patterns to use on the Red and it is easily tied. He has not only caught the above species on it, but also some pretty hefty pike.

WHAT BETTER WAY to end this book than by showing this picture of Kelsey Bell, a new fly fisher, releasing another huge channel cat. She has only been fly fishing for two years, but I have not witnessed another person who has already accomplished what she has. Although she has just started fly-tying, her abilities are out of this world. As of this writing, she has come up with a fantastic shiner pattern that I just can't wait to try and I'm sure it will find a permanent spot in my fly box. Thank you, Kelsey, for allowing me to teach you.

APPENDIX

SPECIES TAKEN ON THE DDH LEECH

The number of different species taken on the DDH (Diamond Dub Holographic) Leech is unreal. This pattern, every time it is used, always seems to bring a new species of fish to hand, whatever country it is fished in. Whether in salt water or freshwater this fly will not disappoint

- rainbow trout
- brown trout
- tiger trout
- brook trout
- splake
- lake trout
- Arctic char
- Dolly varden
- bull trout
- Gila trout
- Yellowstone cutthroat
- westslope cutthroat
- golden trout
- Kamloops trout
- marble trout
- marble and brown hybrid
- coastal cutthroat trout
- Arctic grayling
- steelhead
- lake whitefish
- Rocky mountain whitefish
- Atlantic salmon
- sockeye salmon
- Chinook salmon
- pink salmon
- coho salmon
- chum salmon
- bluegill
- pumpkinseed
- green sunfish
- red breast sunfish
- brown bullhead
- rock bass
- redear sunfish
- black crappie

- white crappie
- longear sunfish
- warmouth
- black-banded sunfish
- banded sunfish
- spotted sunfish
- largemouth bass
- smallmouth bass
- Guadalupe bass
- shoal bass
- redeye bass
- spotted bass
- striped bass
- white bass
- wiper bass
- peacock bass
- muskellunge
- northern pike
- chain pickerel
- redfin pickerel
- tiger musky
- walleye
- sauger
- saugeye
- yellow perch
- white perch
- barramundi
- channel cat
- black bullhead
- freshwater drum
- carp
- big mouth buffalo
- quillback
- goldeye
- mooneye

- pacu
- red tail catfish
- river carp
- giant catfish
- bonefish
- tarpon
- snook
- permit
- kahawai
- redfish
- greenling
- flounder
- barracuda
- grass carp
- sturgeon
- horny head chub
- gar
- blowfish
- trevally
- palometa
- lemon shark
- trigger fish
- stingray
- spotted sea trout
- flathead catfish
- yellow bullhead

183

ESSENTIAL TOOLS FOR BEGINNERS

Most beginners feel that tying tools will cost quite a few dollars which is not the case. When I help people to get started in tying they usually spend $60-80 dollars to purchase the essentials and this will include not only the tools but the hooks and materials for a Woolly Bugger. If a person really enjoys tying upgrading the tools at a later date is what I would recommend.

VICES

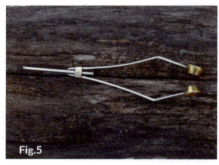

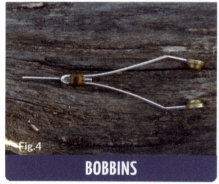

BOBBINS

There are numerous vices on the market with varying prices. Some start at $20 and others will reach $300 to $400, depending on the intricacies of the manufacturer. The vice in Figure 1 is a beginner's vice and will be in the lower price range. With this vice, you do have to adjust the jaws to fit different sizes of hooks. The vice I use, Figure 2, is a Regal. This vice has no hook adjustments because it is spring-loaded. For this advantage, the price of the vice is approximately $250. With the amount of tying I do, it was worth the investment.

If you're a beginner, choose a vice in the price range you can afford. You can always upgrade after you gain some tying experience.

Designed to hold the thread, the bobbin gives the thread tension while tying so you don't have to tie half-hitches while producing the fly. They are a wide variety of bobbins available from a host of different manufacturers. Which one to buy? The one you can afford. Personally I use a flared bobbin: Figure 5. I just feel the thread is more protected from fraying while tying. The straight bobbin, Figure 4, can also be used and it is typically the same price as the flared bobbin.

SCISSORS

Once again, there is a wide variety to choose from, starting at $5 and going up to $45. To start tying, you do not need $45 scissors. What you do need is a pair of scissors that have very fine points, which will enable you to trim the excess material on small flies. This is critical. After you gain some experience, you may want to get a pair of hair scissors to trim deer body hair, or a pair of very fine dry fly scissors. Remember, you are just starting out so for now all you need is one general purpose pair.

When I purchased my scissors they cost $3.95 and I still use them today.

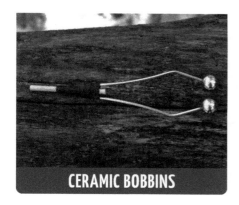

CERAMIC BOBBINS

When using Kevlar or Gel Spun thread, I highly recommend a ceramic bobbin. There is a chance this type of thread can do damage to a regular metal bobbin. When this occurs (and at times you won't know until you keep breaking your thread) it is frustrating because you think you have cheap thread. Instead, there is a groove in the thread tube that you can't get out, resulting in you needing to buy another bobbin. Get the ceramic!

HACKLE PLIERS

These are what I would call a spring type of clamp. They hold the material that you plan to wrap around the hook shank. Usually used with hackle, they can also be used for chenille to hold thread or even tinsel. I have some with straight metal tips, but I find that the material slips out of these pliers. Therefore, I would recommend getting no-slip hackle pliers. I have used these for years with no problems. The price is nice as well: $3 to 5.

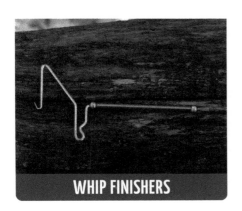

WHIP FINISHERS

Now here is something really interesting. There are a few models of whip finishers out there that I still can't get the hang of, and I've been tying for 55 years. Sad thing, isn't it? Now if they would have had the Matarelli Whip Finisher when I was a kid, I would have kissed the earth and thought my prayers were answered. But I am really glad that Matarelli came out with this fine piece of equipment. Get this type of whip finisher; it will save headaches and broken thread. Highly recommended and easy to use. Price would be $5 to $15.

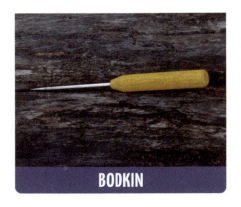

BODKIN

This tool looks a little dangerous and it could be if your small kids get around your bench and decide that it would be fun to poke things. Lesson learned: I got poked a couple of times by my kids! Anyway, this tool's main purpose is to remove your tying mistakes, say, if you wrap some hackle and some fibres get stuck underneath the thread. How would you get those fibres un-trapped? With a bodkin. You can also use a bodkin to apply head cement. Cost is $3 to $5.

HAND DUBBING TWISTER

This tool is required to make dubbing loops (see How to Make a Dubbing Loop, page 188). Depending on the size of loop you want to make, you let out "X" amount of thread. Place the dubbing twister in the middle of the thread and fold the thread back to the hook. Place some dubbing crosswise and twist it in one direction, making a very tight dubbing noodle. It does take a little time to twist the tool but the end results are worth it. This tool costs a few dollars less than a Turbo Twister (below).

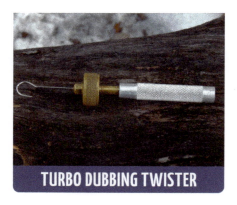

TURBO DUBBING TWISTER

If you do dubbing loops like I do, this tool will save an amazing amount of time. About 10 times faster than the handheld twister, it can create a dubbing noodle in seconds. Cost is around $15.

BATTERY BRUSH

The first time I ever brought this out at a tying demo, I had people laughing. In fact, I had one guy say to me, "Hey my battery terminals need a brushing and my car is only a block away. Can you do it for me?" Well, what can I say, I took the high road and not only showed him but also explained to him why I use a battery brush for dubbing loops. The reason is twofold: first of all, the battery brush gets more loose dubbing out of the dubbing noodle; and second, all the dubbing I take out of the brush I put aside until I get a small bag of it. I then blend it and the colours I get are out of this world—great for getting different colours of dubbing. You will sometimes see the brushes 3 for $1.

HOW TO MAKE A DUBBING LOOP

Dubbing loops are an integral part of tying, it gives the tyer an opportunity to create different bodies for the fly. Also dubbing loops can be used to create the head portion of a streamer.

STEP 1

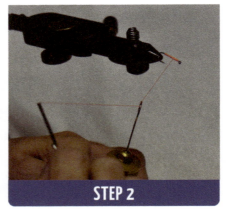

STEP 2

STEP 3

Attach the thread to the vice and ensure it is secure.

Let out some thread, the length depends on the amount of hook shank you have to cover. Place the dubbing twister in the middle of the thread.

Fold the thread back up to the hook shank.

STEP 4

STEP 5

STEP 6

Wrap the thread around the open end of the loop effectively closing the top of the loop.

Place the dubbing in the loop crosswise.

Twist the loop tight.

Brush out the loose fibres.

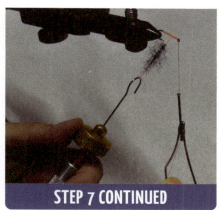

This is what the dubbing noodle looks like after brushing.

Wrap the dubbing noodle.

Tie off the dubbing noodle. The dubbing loop is complete.

HOW TO CARD YARN

Carding yarn is one of the easiest things to do and doing this will give the fly tyer a distinct advantage in tying different baitfish or attractor patterns. The colours are limitless and so are the flies that can be tied.

STEP 1

Cut 10 pieces of yarn that are 10 inches (25.5 cm) in length

STEP 2

Knot all 10 pieces together. Ensure the knot is in the middle of the pieces.

STEP 3

With a cat brush start to separate the tips of the yarn

STEP 3 CONTINUED

This is what the yarn should look like after the tips are brushed out

STEP 4

Continue working the brush through the yarn fibers slowly making your way to the knot.

STEP 5

The finished carded yarn.

EXAMPLE

A selection of different colours. The great thing about doing yarn like this is that any colour of yarn can be carded giving the tier a limitless choice of colours for the different flies that can be tied.

GLOSSARY

Angora: A type of dubbing that comes from angora goats. If cut in the proper length, it is a great substitute for seal's fur.

Anti-static bag: A bag that is used to store electronic components. This bag can be cut to different widths to use for wing cases or bodies on flies.

Antron: Made up from tri-lobal filaments that will reflect light. Can be used for dry fly wings, wing cases, or as a tailing material.

Bernat Boa: A type of wool that can be found anywhere wool is sold. Comes in a variety of colours.

Chenille: A type of wool that has smaller fibres twisted together with two core strings, which give this wool a type of caterpillar look. It has been use since the mid 1800s to tie flies.

Chenille, crystal: Made the same way as chenille, it contains pearlescent fibres, giving more flash to the finished fly.

Chenille, polar: This wool has very long translucent fibres, which will undulate in the water making this an ideal product for doing bodies on flies.

Chenille, rayon: A woven type of wool that has pearlescent fibres, which blend in to produce a bit of flash.

Chenille, Ultra: Has very short fibres that makes this wool feel like suede. Ideal for making extended bodies on dry flies.

Chenille, velvet: Similar to **Ultra chenille** (see above), but very tightly wound and therefore stiffer.

Coq de Leon: A type of fowl that has a terrific mottled pattern on the feathers. These feathers are usually from a hen as opposed to a rooster. The feathers can come from the neck area or from the base of the tail.

Craft fur: A synthetic material that imitates natural fur. Some fly shops carry this product, but you can also find it at hobby stores.

Krystal Flash: A flash material that is twisted 360 degrees so the light can reflect all the way around. Great material for tails or wings on streamers to give the fly a baitfish flash.

Darkwater Dubbing: This is my own dubbing, which I make and sell. (www.darkwaterdubbing.wordpress.com) Typically, the rabbit fibres are much longer than commercial brands. If unavailable, just about any dubbing will do.

Diamond Brite: This dubbing by Hareline Dubbin, Inc. is made from long, synthetic fibres. It gives off a bit of flash in the brightness, which you sometimes need in a fly.

Dubbing noodle: A dubbing loop that has been loaded with dubbing and spun tight, or a strand of thread that is covered with dubbing.

Deer body hair: The hair from the body of a deer. This hair is excellent for spinning around the hook shank.

Extreme String: It has long wool like fibres that are 1.5 in (40 mm) long and mixed in with those fibres are a metallic, reflective tinsel.

Flashabou: A flash material that is in 10 in (25.4 cm) in length and is usually added onto tails of pike flies or used in wings on streamers.

Goose (Turkey) biots: These shorter and smaller feathers come from the leading edge of a goose's (or turkey's) primary flight feathers located on the wing. They come in dyed colours that you have to purchase from a fly shop.

Hackle: This comes from two different locations on a rooster: the neck area is where the hackle cape is located, and the saddle hackle comes from the back area close to the tail. These feathers when applied to the hook and then wrapped around the shank will be splayed out. Hens also have hackle but that is classified as soft hackle.

Hackle stems: Hackle stems are just that: what is left over after you strip the fibres off the feather. Great tail-making material.

Midge flex: A narrower type of stretch material than **scud back** (see below). Ideal for making bodies on small flies and creating legs on a mayfly nymph.

Marabou: This feather originally came from a marabou stork, but nowadays comes from a turkey. These are the immature feathers that are found on a turkey, which can be dyed any colour.

Ostrich herl: The two natural colours of ostrich are black (males) and grey (females). Their body feathers are soft and downy with a very thick stem. The fibres that come off the stem is what is referred to as "herl," which is used in the tying of bodies, tails, and wing cases.

Peacock herl: Fibres from the tail of a peacock. The tail feathers have a very thick stem and it is the individual fibres that we, as fly tyers, are interested in. This herl can be used for streamer wings, making bodies, and forming wing cases.

Philoplume feather: This feather is located underneath the rump feather of a pheasant. It will always be a natural grey colour.

Polar dub: A synthetic dubbing material that has UV flash added in it.

Pheasant rump feather: The bluish-green feathers that are found on the very rear portion of the ring-necked pheasant's back close to the rump of the bird.

Quill: Comes from the wings of different birds. Most commonly used are turkey and goose quills. Whether they are primary or secondary flight feathers makes no difference in tying fishing flies. In tying traditional salmon patterns, it *does* make a difference with most tyers using the secondary quills.

Rib: A material that is tied in at the rear of the hook and is spaced out evenly when wrapped giving the illusion of a segmented body. A hackle feather can also be used as a rib; a good example is the Easter Egg Bugger (p. 93).

Scud back: A wider strip of latex, which is also thinner than **midge flex** (see above), and used in making a body of a fly or for a wing case.

Swiss straw: Also known as raffia, this material is an excellent choice for making wing cases or doing scud backs. Virtually impossible to rip crosswise but it can be easily separated lengthwise.

Whip finish: The finishing knot on the fly. This is the last tying step in completing any fly. If you search the internet for "whip finish knot," there are some excellent how-to videos on the subject.

Wing case: The best way to describe this is: an immature aquatic insect carries its adult wings on top of its back like a school kid carrying a backpack. As the insect matures, the wing case gets darker.

Mayflies, stoneflies, and other insects all have wing cases. As fly tyers, we mimic this by using a quill or other material.

Zonker strips: A vertically cut rabbit hide in the same direction of the hair, cut 1/4 inch (6mm) wide. Fantastic for making backs on minnow or leech patterns.

Zonker strips, crosscut: Rabbit hide horizontally cut, perpendicular to the direction of the hair. The strips are 1/4 in (6 mm) wide and can be tied in and wrapped like a piece of **chenille** (see above).

FINAL THOUGHTS

As you may have noticed throughout the book, at the end of some of the tying sequences, I supplied the species of fish that particular fly has caught. It is not written in stone that these are the only fish this pattern can take: every fly can take multiple species of fish if you want to experiment and have fun. Let me relate this story to you.

I was sitting at a table, during a lunch break, tying a few flies. A co-worker came over, sat down across from me, and watched me tie flies. Of course, a conversation was struck and he stated that he was a fly fisher, but since moving to Winnipeg he had not taken out his fly rod.

"Why not"? I asked.

"There's no trout around here," he said.

I started to chuckle and he gave me a quizzical look. "Don't need trout to go fly fishing," I said.

Once again the quizzical look, so I suggested to him that fly fishing the Red River is a challenge that everyone should try. So we made plans to meet up at the town of Lockport the next evening. Once there he looked at the water and shook his head.

"That water looks so muddy nothing could live there," he said.

"Trust me," I said. "We'll have a blast."

I rigged up the rods and tied a Rebecca's Damsel (page 16) on each of them. My buddy got an olive fly while I got a pale green one. While walking down to the water's edge, I explained to him about how carp feed and what they feed on. Rebecca's Damsel is one of those patterns that can imitate virtually any nymph that lives in the water, from damsel flies to mayflies. And wouldn't you know it, we timed everything perfectly. The carp were in the shallows tailing and feeding on nymphs.

Well, it didn't take long for him to tie into a carp and boy was he excited. He was having a blast. Now, when I take people out to the Red I usually don't start fishing until they land a few fish. At this stage of my life, I have more fun watching other people catch fish than catching them myself. So after landing his sixth carp, he asked if I was going to fish.

"Yep," I said. "In the next couple of minutes."

I moved down a ways and started to cast. The dry line lay down perfectly and I was concentrating on where the line and leader meet. The line twitched and I set the hook. The fish took off and zigzagged across the river. I knew I didn't have a carp but rather a channel cat. Yep, a channel cat that was 37 ¾ in (95.88 cm), on a size 14 Rebecca's Damsel. What a thrill! So if you want to have fun, try the different species with these flies. It will surprise you!

If you take a close look in the mouth of this channel cat, the picture on the previous page, you will see a size 14 Rebecca's Damsel. What a fight. I never thought a fish like that would take such a small fly but, of course, there are always lessons to be learned.

INDEX—CHRONOLOGICAL ORDER

CHIRONOMIDS

R & B Tom 2
Red Tom 3
Clear Tom 4
Summer Duck Chironomid 5
Fur Midge 7
Stu's Orange Chromie (Bonus Fly 1) 9
Stu's Chromie 10
CB Midge Black 11
CB Midge Wire 12
Red Bead Midge 13

NYMPHS

Rebecca's Damsel 16
Darkwater Damsel 17
'52 Buick 18
Jen Dragon 19
Bodacious Dragon Fly Nymph 20
Huff 'n Fluff Dragon 22
Darkwater Swimmer 23
Nixon's Nymph 24
Stu's Backswimmer 25
Floating Backswimmer 26
(Bonus fly 2)
Abbott's Costello 28
Owen's Golden Retriever 29
Elastic Band Caddis 30
FFA Caddis Emerger 32
Manitoba Mayfly 33
Cheater's Caddis 34
FFA Stonefly 36
Derek's Demon Stone 38
Corrigan's Craw 40
The Muncher 43
Calli Nymph 45
Stu's Sow Bug 47
The Tick 48
Beck's Hex 50

WET FLIES

Mark's Pink Bead Fly 54
Sally Soft Hackle 55
GH Wet Fly 56
Grouse and Orange 57
Grouse and Green 58
Mrs. Simpson 60
Drunken Nymph 61

DRY FLIES

Mike's Mayfly 64
Mike's Parachute Mayfly 66
Mike's Hexagenia 68

POPPERS

Mikey Mouse 72
Steve's Slider 74
The Leaf 75
SE Foam Popper 76
Tiger's Tail Popper 78
Jig-A-Pop 80
Kermit 82
The Terminator 84
Bass Diver 85

STREAMERS

The Blob 88
Becky's Black Strip Leech 90
(Bonus fly 3)
Pink Zonker 91
Easter Egg Bugger 93
Sawich Killer 94
Claret Tiger Leech 96
Myminnow 97
DeRose Dace 98
Mallard SB 100
Bendback Minnow Black and Orange 103
Whatizit 104

Erickson's Clouser   105
Kevin's Leech   106
(Bonus fly 4)
Tokaryk Killer   107
DDH Leech   109
Red River Shiner   110
SRT Stickleback   111
Bou Bug   112
Erickson's Dream   114
Stu's Sculpin   116
Zeke's Nightmare   118
Brigiette's Badass Baitfish   121
Manitoba Matuka   122
Rolled Muddler   123
Lockport Standard   124
DDH Eyes Natural Grey   125
DDH Eyes White Minnow   128
DDH Head Purple and Pink   130

PIKE AND MUSKY STREAMERS

CG's Minnow   134
Hillbilly Baba   135
TGT Streamer   136
Bunny Leech   137
Green Zacattack   138
Red River Sculpin   140
P & W Pike Muddler   143
Weedman's Slider   144
Winter's Storm   146
(Bonus fly 5)
KT's Baitfish   148
Zonker Minnow Perch   150
Super Cisco   152
Perch Zacattack   156
SR Yellow Red Head   158
Black and Chartreuse Casper   160
Mike's Goldfish   162
Rain Drop   164

RC's Punch Fly   166
Sinfield's Musky Killer   168
Sinfield's Zonker   170
TJ's Folly   173
TJ's Folly Two   174
Craft Fur Popsicle   176
Keith's Flatwing Streamer   178
Steve's Sheep Deceiver   179

INDEX—ALPHABETICAL ORDER

'52 Buick   18

A

Abbott's Costello   28

B

Bass Diver   85
Beck's Hex   50
Becky's Black Strip Leech (Bonus fly 3)   90
Bend Back Minnow Black and Orange   103
Bodacious Dragon Fly Nymph   20
'Bou Bug   112
Brigitte's Badass Baitfish   121
Bunny Leech   137

C

Calli Nymph   45
Casper   160
CB Midge Black   11
CB Midge Wire   12
CG's Minnow   134
Cheater's Caddis   34
Claret Tiger Leech   96
Corrigan's Craw   40
Craft Fur Popsicle   176

D

Darkwater Damsel   17
Darkwater Swimmer   23
DDH Eyes Natural Grey   125
DDH Eyes White Minnow   128
DDH Head Pink and Purple   130
DDH Leech   109
DeRose Dace   98
Derek's Demon Stone   38
Drunken Nymph   61

E

Easter Egg Bugger   93
Elastic Band Caddis   30
Erickson's Clouser   105
Erickson's Dream   114

F

FFA Caddis Emerger   32
FFA Stonefly   36
Floating Backswimmer (Bonus fly 2)   26
Fur Midge   7

G

GH Wet Fly   56
Grouse and Green   58
Grouse and Orange   57

H

Hillbilly Baba   135
Huff 'N Fluff Dragon   22

J

Jen Dragon   19
Jig-A-Pop   80

K

Keith's Flatwing Streamer   178
Kermit   82
Kevin's Leech (Bonus fly 4)   106
KT's Baitfish   148

L

Lockport Standard   124

M

Mallard SB   100
Manitoba Matuka   122
Manitoba Mayfly   33
Mark's Pink Bead Fly   54
Mikey Mouse   72
Mike's Goldfish   162
Mike's Hexagenia   68
Mike's Mayfly   64
Mike's Parachute Mayfly   66
Mrs. Simpson   60
Myminnow   97

N
Nixon's Nymph   24

O
Owen's Golden Retriever   29

P
Pike Muddler Pink and White   143

R
Rain Drop   164
RC's Punch Fly   166
Rebecca's Damsel   16
Red Bead Midge   13
Red River Sculpin   140
Red River Shiner   110
Rolled Muddler   123

S
Sally Soft Hackle   55
Sawich Killer   94
SE Foam Popper   76
Sinfield's Musky Killer   168
Sinfield's Zonker   170
SRT Stickleback   111
SR Yellow Red Head   158
Steve's Sheep Deceiver   179
Steve's Slider   74
Stu's Backswimmer   25
Stu's Chromie   10
Stu's Orange Chromie (Bonus fly 1)   9
Stu's Sculpin   116
Stu's Sow Bug   47
Summer Duck Chironomid   5
Super Cisco   152

T
TGT Streamer   136

The Blob   88
The Leaf   75
The Muncher   43
The Terminator   84
The Tick   48
Tiger's Tail Popper   78
TJ's Folly   173
TJ's Folly Two   174
Tokaryk Killer   107
Tom Clear   4
Tom R & B   2
Tom Red   3

W
Weedman's Slider   144
Whatizit   104
Winter's Storm (Bonus fly 5)   146

Z
Zacattack Green   138
Zacattack Perch   156
Zeke's Nightmare   118
Zonker Minnow   150
Zonker Pink   91

CPSIA information can be obtained
at www.ICGtesting.com
Printed in the USA
BVHW051444211021
619346BV00002B/3